W9-CYU-975

Bird of a Different Feather

100 Recipes to Entertain at Home

Esther Gerhard

Impact Press
Newtown Square, PA

Library of Congress Cataloging-in-Publication Data

Gerhard, Esther
   Bird of a Different Feather / 100 Recipes to Entertain at Home / Esther Gerhard
   ISBN 09671825-3-0
DNLM/DLC   99-96301
for Library of Congress   CIP

©1999 by Esther Gerhard

Printed in the United States of America. All rights reserved. Except as permitted under the Copyright Act of 1976, no part of this publication may be reproduced or distributed in any form or by any means, or stored in a data base or retrieval system, without the prior written permission of the publisher.

To my dear friend Ursi Bächi, a musician in and out of the kitchen, with whom I spent many memorable meals and who left us far too soon.

Acknowledgments

I thank my family and friends, without whose encouragement I could not have completed this book. Special thanks go to Barbara Halpern and Ellen Frohwirth, who tested the recipes with great care and made valuable suggestions. Affection and thanks to Marina Hoffman, Siraik Zakarian, Shirley Hallam, and Ken Bookman for their editorial help.

eg

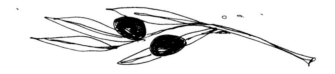

Cooking is my way of expressing affection, of drawing people closer and seeing them happy.

I start thinking about a dish from the moment I see fresh ingredients at a farmer's market. Nowadays, I rarely cook from recipes. It wasn't always that easy for me. There was a time when I, too, had to follow a recipe meticulously, constantly practicing my skills to gain the experience that would lead me to develop a personal cooking style.

You, too, will develop a distinctive style that reflects your preferences for certain ingredients and flavors. But first you must become familiar with the techniques. If you enjoy cooking, this will not be difficult, but it will take you a while to get there. If you are new to cooking, limit yourself to a few recipes and prepare them over and over—until you are satisfied with the result. Don't let the occasional goof discourage you, and keep in mind that you are your own best teacher. Like all crafts, cooking requires perseverance and can be mastered only with practice and experience.

Contents

Poultry
1

Vegetables
111

Soups
48

Grains
83

Appetizers
62

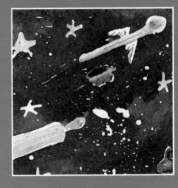

Desserts
133

Glossary   *166*

Index   *168*

Basics
152

Preface

Poultry has been a favored food for centuries and in recent years has become increasingly popular among consumers looking for maximum nutrition with minimum fat. And for people who are concerned about eating meats from animals that may have been treated with antibiotics, preservatives, and growth hormones, there are now organically grown, free-range and naturally raised poultry of all varieties. The new growing methods result in a fresher tasting product with far better flavor and texture.

These developments inspired me to take a new approach in the preparation of poultry, and I hope the following recipes reflect my enthusiasm for these delicious, wholesome foods.

To complement the poultry dishes, the accompanying grains and vegetables needed a new approach as well. In addition to using basic staples such as yellow corn, grits, and barley, I have experimented with new products such as quinoa and kashi. Because grains are an important part of our diet, I want them to taste as exciting as possible so I have added spices such as cardamom, cloves, and caraway and flavorings such as orange, pistachios, and mint.

You'll notice that smoked salmon dominates the appetizer section. That's because it reflects my personal taste for combining fish with salads, vegetables, and pasta. The recipes for salmon wrapped in seaweed and the cucumber wheels with crabmeat were influenced by Japanese sushi cooking.

I have tried to present the recipes in a logical sequence, and all of them are relatively simple to prepare. Just be sure to allow enough time to follow the procedures step by step.

It was a pleasure to create these recipes, and nothing would please me more than to know that some of these dishes turned one of your ordinary meals into a festive occasion.

Esther Gerhard
Philadelphia, August 1999

Poultry

The beauty of poultry lies in its simplicity and its versatility. Duck is probably a little more finicky about the company it keeps than chicken or turkey, but if you're making a main course out of poultry, you've got far more cooking possibilities than you could ever try in a long lifetime.

So do it right. There aren't many rules, but help yourself by taking a few minutes to learn about buying and cooking your poultry. You and your guests will be glad you did.

First, let's talk a little about buying. As you might suspect, freshness is all-important, and that's where a reputable poultry purveyor can help. For one thing, the purveyor can help you select your poultry. But he or she can also meet special requests for removing bones, skin, and tendons.

That doesn't mean you can't get good poultry from a supermarket case. Just know what you're seeing. If chicken breasts are packaged, check for freshness by pressing lightly with your thumb, and if the flesh springs back, the product is fresh. Accumulated liquid in packaged breasts means the product has been frozen, which is fine as long as you are using them by the date indicated on the package. If, however, you plan to freeze an extra portion, the product has to be fresh.

Once you have established freshness, buy several portions and freeze the extras in special freezer bags that are tightly sealed. The recommended storage time for chicken breasts is three months, but I detect a deterioration in the flavor and color after just one month, so I never keep them much longer than that. Always thaw frozen poultry in its wrapper in the refrigerator. A two-pound package of skinless, boneless chicken breasts will need 24 hours to defrost.

Whether the poultry you buy is called free-range, all-natural, organic, or traditionally raised, it's important to follow the recipe's indicated cooking times so you'll get a moist and delicate result.

The biggest problem in cooking whole chickens is that white meat is finished cooking before dark meat, so a perfectly cooked breast might sit next to a seriously underdone leg. That's why I don't like to cook whole chickens. Although you want the chicken fully cooked, that doesn't mean you have to overcook it. To have more control over cooking the breast meat, I cut it into slices to help the breast cook more even. Thus cooked, they provide a marvelous foil for any number of flavored sauces.

The beginning of this section offers some basic cooking methods. Nothing fancy, just simple and delicious poultry, garnished with a sprig of fresh herb or served on a bed of salad greens. The rest of the chapter has recipes for a more ambitious presentation.

If you are grilling the poultry, use an old-fashioned, well-seasoned cast-iron frying pan. Such pans retain heat well, cook at very high temperatures, and produce a crust. But switch to a nonstick skillet or enamel-coated pan if your sauce is made with acidic ingredients.

Whenever poultry is cooked in the oven, the accuracy of your oven temperature is important to guarantee the given cooking times. An inexpensive oven thermometer is the best tool for that task.

Although this cookbook is not geared to microwave cooking and no conversions of cooking times and temperatures are given, creative cooks with limited time and more experience with microwave energy can cook parts of these recipes with this technology.

I made all the poultry sauces in this book with homemade stocks that I reduced to a concentrated base called a demi-glace. The majority of recipes use no flour or starch for thickening the sauce, which is why they're so light. You can find commercial demi-glace in specialty stores and some supermarkets.

Despite its bad reputation, salt remains a necessity in my cooking. Adding it to a dish opens up the flavors and blends them harmoniously. Personal taste for salt differs, so taste foods—and consider your guests—before adding any.

Although most of the sauces are made without flour, dredging the poultry pieces in flour prior to sautéing will help you avoid splatters.

Some common-sense precautions are needed when working with raw chicken. Wash the cutting board and knife with soap and warm water before using it for other foods.

■

The usual serving size is about 6 ounces and all the recipes here call for poultry without skin. That's one way I've reduced fat. Another is that skillets with nonstick surfaces permit cooking with less butter or oil.

When I use butter, it's unsalted, and if possible, I've substituted canola, safflower, or olive oil. If you need to further reduce fat, poaching, boiling, or grilling will help.

Poultry Parts

Chicken filet mignon refers to the small strips from boned, skinned chicken breasts. They may be sold as breast tenders, chicken fingers, chicken filets, or chicken stir-fry.

Chicken thighs are the upper part of the leg without the drumstick.

Turkey tenderloin is the inner part of the breast.

The breast of the turkey is also sold as turkey broil because it resembles a London broil cut of beef.

Turkey chops are cut from the turkey breast but instead of cutting them thin and long, they are cut across into 1-inch-thick slices.

All these cuts have tendons. The white band connecting the breast muscle to the bone must be removed before cooking.

Grilled Chicken Breasts

A cast-iron grill pan, with raised ridges lets you duplicate the effect of an oven, but with greater control. You'll be able to omit the use of additional oil and still sear the breasts to perfection.

Makes 6 servings

6 chicken breast halves, skin and bones
    removed, about 6 ounces each
2 tablespoons olive oil, approximately
Freshly ground black pepper to taste
2 tablespoons soy sauce

Remove the tendons from the chicken breasts and cut each piece in half horizontally. Brush lightly on both sides with olive oil, sprinkle with pepper, and drizzle with soy sauce.

Heat a large cast-iron ridged skillet on the stovetop until it's smoking. Brush the ridges lightly with olive oil, add the chicken pieces, 3 a time, and brown for 1 minute. Rotate 180 degrees, and brown for 30 seconds more. Turn the chicken and repeat on the other side. Transfer the browned chicken to a plate, cover with aluminum foil, and cook the remaining chicken breasts in the same manner.

Note: These breasts can be served over salad greens. Or they can be accompanied by any sauce from other recipes in this chapter. Or you can drizzle a bit of olive oil and lemon juice over the chicken and place roasted peppers, cucumbers, or tomato slices between the chicken slices and accompany with crusty bread.

Poached Chicken Breasts

Poaching is one of the best ways to cook a chicken breast with maximum flavor yet minimum calories.

Makes 6 servings

6 chicken breast halves, skin and bones removed, about 6 ounces each
½ teaspoon salt
1 teaspoon freshly ground black pepper
4 cups Chicken Stock (page 155), Mushroom Stock (page 159), or Vegetable Stock (page 164)
½ cup dry white wine

Remove tendons from the chicken breasts and sprinkle them with the salt and pepper. Place the chicken between sheets of wax paper and pound lightly to an even thickness with a rolling pin.

Simmer the stock and wine in a large saucepan for 5 minutes. Add 3 of the chicken breasts, simmer for 4 minutes, turn the breasts, and simmer for 4 minutes more. (Be sure the breasts are submerged for the entire cooking time.) Transfer the chicken to a plate, and cover. Return the stock to the boil, and cook the remaining chicken breasts in the same manner.

Transfer to a plate, spoon a bit of the stock on top, and cover with aluminum foil. Strain the stock and store in the refrigerator or freezer for future use.

Note: Serve in any of several ways. You can serve the breasts as described here, cut horizontally into thin slices with some stock spooned on top, garnished with minced scallions, and arranged on salad greens. Or you can make a soup by simmering pieces of your favorite vegetable in the poaching liquid, cutting the cooked chicken breasts into cubes, and adding the chicken to the stock with the vegetable. Or you can serve this chicken with any sauce in this book used for cold chicken breasts.

Sautéed Chicken Breasts

There's no quicker way to cook a chicken breast than in a hot skillet. But make sure the oil is hot enough to cook the chicken without being absorbed.

Makes 6 servings

6 chicken breast halves, skin and bones removed, about 6 ounces each
1 teaspoon soy sauce
1 tablespoon freshly ground black pepper
¼ cup fresh tarragon, minced
¼ cup flour
¼ cup canola or safflower oil
1 tablespoon fresh lemon juice
Tarragon sprigs, for garnish

Remove tendons from the chicken breasts, cut each piece horizontally into three slices, and sprinkle with the soy sauce and pepper. Press the tarragon into the chicken slices and dredge the pieces in the flour.

Heat 2 tablespoons of the oil in a large frying pan until very hot, shake off any excess flour, and brown the chicken slices, in batches of 4, over medium heat for 30 seconds on each side. Set aside and cover with aluminum foil. Add a bit more oil to the frying pan and repeat with the second batch. Repeat until all the chicken is done. After half the chicken is cooked, wipe the pan with paper towels, add the remaining oil, and continue cooking the remaining slices. Drizzle with the lemon juice and serve garnished with tarragon sprigs.

Whole Boiled Chicken

This slow-cooking method produces moist and delicate meat throughout. It is important, though, not to let the chicken stand for more than five hours after the initial cooking, to remove it promptly after the second cooking, and to discard the cooking liquid.

Makes 3 or 4 servings

***1 frying chicken, weighing not more than
    3½ pounds***

Remove the giblets and neck from the cavity of the chicken, and thoroughly rinse the bird inside and out with cold water. In an 8-quart or larger stockpot, bring to a rolling boil enough water to cover the chicken. Add the chicken, making sure it is completely submerged. Return the water to the boil, and cook for 5 minutes. Turn off the heat, cover the pot, and let stand for 5 hours.

Return the water to a rolling boil, turn off the heat, and let stand, covered, for 4 more hours.

Remove the chicken and discard the cooking liquid. Remove the skin, bones, and fatty parts of the bird, and cut into bite-size pieces. Use with any sauce from the recipes for cold chicken breasts.

Chicken Breasts with Artichokes, Green Peppercorns, and Pastry Hearts

One reason chicken is so popular is that it has an affinity for so many ingredients, including assertive ones, such as those in this recipe. Advance preparation makes this dish easy for company, and the pastry hearts add lots of eye appeal.

Makes 6 servings

6 chicken breast halves, skin and bones removed, about 6 ounces each
Salt and freshly ground black pepper to taste
2 tablespoons lemon juice
1 tablespoon fresh green peppercorns in brine, drained
1 sheet (9 x 9½ inches) frozen puff pastry
1 egg yolk
1 teaspoon water
5 tablespoons butter
1 can (8 ounces drained weight) artichoke hearts in brine
2 cups Chicken Stock (page 155)
¼ cup homemade crème fraîche (page 157) or heavy cream

Remove tendons from chicken breasts and sprinkle them with salt, pepper and half the lemon juice. Measure the green peppercorns into a plastic bag, close the bag, and pound with a rolling pin to crush the peppercorns. Divide the crushed peppercorns among the chicken breasts, and press them into the surface. Set aside.

Preheat oven to 375°F.

Defrost the puff pastry by letting it sit at room temperature for about 20 minutes. Unfold and cut along the perforations. Using a heart-shaped cookie cutter or a cardboard template, cut out 12 hearts. Beat the egg and the water with a fork, and brush the hearts with the egg wash. Be careful not to touch the edges with the egg, or you'll prevent the puff pastry from rising. Bake on a cookie sheet for 10 minutes. Place on a rack to cool.

In a large nonstick frying pan, melt 2 tablespoons of the butter and brown half the chicken breasts, peppercorn side down, over moderate heat for 2 minutes per side. Add another 2 tablespoons of butter and brown the remaining chicken breasts. Set aside and cover with wax paper.

Drain the artichoke hearts, rinse briefly with cold water, and cut each into eighths. Melt the remaining 1 tablespoon of butter in the same frying pan and cook the artichoke pieces over low heat for 5 minutes, stirring occasionally. Add the Chicken Stock, and boil for 10 minutes. Taste and add remaining lemon juice and additional salt and pepper. Stir in the *crème fraîche* or cream, and simmer until lightly thickened.

Just before serving, reheat the sauce, add the chicken breasts and juices to warm briefly, and serve the breasts with the sauce spooned on top and garnished with the pastry hearts.

Chicken Breasts
with Black Currants and Pink Peppercorns

When a sweet flavor marries a spice, it has to be done subtly. I use black currant preserves because the sugar in the preserves diminishes the astringent flavor of the black currants. Tellicherry peppercorns are larger than regular black peppercorns because they have been left on the vine longer. The extra ripening time gives them a richer flavor.

Makes 6 servings

6 chicken breast halves, skin and bones
      removed, about 6 ounces each
Salt to taste
1 tablespoon pink peppercorns
1 tablespoon tellicherry peppercorns
¼ cup flour
¼ cup safflower oil, approximately
2 cups Chicken Stock (page 155)
½ cup black currant preserves
Lemon juice to taste
Fresh thyme sprigs, for garnish

Remove the tendons from the chicken breasts and cut each piece horizontally into three thin slices. Spread the pieces on wax paper and sprinkle lightly with salt. Combine and grind the two peppercorns, and sprinkle evenly over the chicken pieces. Cover with another sheet of wax paper, and, with a rolling pin, press firmly to make the peppercorns adhere to chicken.

Dredge the chicken pieces in the flour. In a large nonstick skillet, heat 2 tablespoons of the safflower oil. Shake off any excess flour and brown the chicken over moderate to high heat in batches of three for 30 seconds per side. Transfer the chicken pieces to a plate and cover loosely with aluminum foil. Wipe the pan with paper towels and add more oil as needed before browning the remaining pieces.

Add the Chicken Stock, bring to the boil, and reduce volume by half. Stir in the preserves, season with additional salt and lemon juice, and return the chicken pieces to reheat gently. Fan three pieces of chicken on each of 6 preheated plates, spoon some sauce on top, and garnish with fresh thyme sprigs.

Chicken Breasts with Capers and Pimientos

This is a tasty recipe for last-minute guests and a good example of why you should always have a package of chicken breasts in the freezer. Capers and pimientos are sitting in most pantries anyway, so put them to work here.

Makes 6 servings

*6 scallions, white parts with 2 inches of
    greens, roots trimmed*
*6 chicken breast halves, skin and bones
    removed, about 6 ounces each*
Salt to taste
½ teaspoon freshly ground black pepper
1 tablespoon olive oil
6 strips bacon
½ cup Madeira wine
2 cups Chicken Stock (page 155)
¼ cup nonpareil capers, drained
*1 jar (4 ounces) pimientos, drained and
    cut into thin strips*

Preheat the broiler to high.

Use a sharp knife to cut down the green part of each scallion, taking care not to cut all the way through the white bulb. The goal is to make a "brush" that will hold together. Make as many fine cuts as possible and place in ice water for 20 minutes or until the cut parts open.

Remove the tendons from the chicken breasts, sprinkle both sides with salt and pepper, brush with the olive oil, and place each piece, without overlapping, in a broiler pan.

Brown the bacon strips in a frying pan until crisp, and drain the strips on paper towels. Discard all but 2 tablespoons of the bacon fat and add the Madeira. Cook over high heat until the liquid has been reduced to 1 tablespoon. Add the Chicken Stock, capers, and minced pimientos, and simmer the sauce for 2 minutes. Season to taste with additional salt and pepper.

Broil the chicken breasts 4 inches from the heat for 3 minutes per side. Place the cooked breasts on a cutting board, cover with aluminum foil, and let sit for 10 minutes. Cut the breasts on the bias into ½-inch pieces and place them briefly in the sauce to reheat. Arrange 1 chicken breast on each of 6 dinner plates, cover with some sauce, crumble 1 slice of bacon over each portion, and garnish each with a scallion "brush."

Chicken Breasts
with Cornmeal Rounds and Tomato Sauce

Hearty dishes don't have to be heavy. And when they're built around chicken, they usually aren't. Cornmeal rounds and tomato sauce do the trick in this dish, and you won't need any side dishes, either.

Makes 6 servings

*6 chicken breast halves, skin and bones
    removed, about 6 ounces each*
*Salt and freshly ground black pepper to
    taste*
1 tablespoon lemon juice
6 fresh basil leaves
¾ cup flour
5 tablespoons grated Parmesan cheese
3 large eggs
1 pound green beans, tips removed
4 to 6 tablespoons canola oil
*3 cups Three-in-One Tomato Sauce (page
    163), any style*
*12 cornmeal rounds (use the recipe for
    Cornmeal Hearts with Maple-Glazed
    Onions on page 91, but make only
    the cornmeal pieces and cut them
    into rounds, not hearts)*

Remove the tendons from the chicken breasts, cut each piece horizontally into 2 slices, place on wax paper, and sprinkle lightly with salt, pepper, and lemon juice. Top each piece with a basil leaf, cover with wax paper, and pound lightly.

Place the flour and Parmesan cheese into a mixing bowl. Beat the eggs with a fork and stir into the flour to make a batter.

Bring about 3 quarts of salted water to a boil and cook the green beans in the boiling water for 5 minutes. Drain the beans, plunge them into ice water, and set them aside.

Heat 2 tablespoons of the oil in a large frying pan. Dip the chicken pieces in the batter to coat lightly, and brown the pieces 4 at a time over medium heat for 3 minutes per side. Wipe the pan clean and add more oil between batches.

Heat the tomato sauce and cornmeal rounds. (Both can be heated in a microwave oven.) Place the beans vertically and horizontally on each of 6 dinner plates, forming a grid pattern. Center 2 cornmeal hearts on the beans and top each heart with a piece of chicken. Spoon some tomato sauce over and pass the remaining sauce at the table.

Chicken Breasts
with Curry Sauce, Dates, and Grapefruit

This is a dish of contrasts, with radically different tastes everywhere. The dates are sweet, the grapefruit tart, the curry peppery—and the chicken a perfect vehicle for them all.

Makes 6 servings

2 large pink grapefruits
½ cup heavy cream
6 chicken breast halves, skin and bones
*   removed, about 6 ounces each*
Salt to taste
¼ cup flour
4 tablespoons (½ stick) butter
3 tablespoons shallots, minced
3 medium cloves garlic, minced
3 tablespoons sweet curry powder
*   (Madras brand)*
1 cup Chicken Stock (page 155)
1 tablespoon lemon juice
½ cup dates, pitted and quartered

Remove the skin and white pith from the grapefruits, divide each one into wedges, and refrigerate. Whip the heavy cream and refrigerate.

Remove the tendons from the chicken breasts, and cut each piece horizontally into 3 slices. Sprinkle lightly with salt, and dredge each piece in the flour. Melt 1 tablespoon of the butter in a large nonstick frying pan, and cook the chicken pieces in three batches over moderate heat for 30 seconds per side. Set aside the cooked pieces and keep them warm. Wipe the pan between batches and melt another 1 tablespoon of butter before browning the next batch of chicken pieces.

When all the chicken is cooked, wipe the frying pan with a paper towel, melt the remaining tablespoon of butter, cook the shallots and garlic until soft, then add the curry powder. Increase the heat and cook, stirring, until the curry becomes very fragrant. Add the Chicken Stock and the lemon juice, and simmer for 15 minutes. Season to taste with additional salt.

Divide the chicken pieces among 6 dinner plates, bring the sauce to a boil, turn off the heat, and add the dates and the whipped cream. Spoon the sauce over the chicken, and serve immediately, garnished with the grapefruit segments.

Chicken Breasts with Ginger and Lime

Ginger and lime combine for a unique taste sensation that the chicken carries off perfectly. I prefer the bold flavor of the mature tellicherry pepper in this recipe, but freshly ground black pepper works well, too.

Makes 6 servings

6 chicken breast halves, skin and bones removed, about 6 ounces each
1 teaspoon salt
½ teaspoon ground tellicherry pepper
6 tablespoons butter
¼ cup dry white vermouth
3 cups Beef Stock (page 152)
2 tablespoon freshly grated gingerroot
2 tablespoons fresh lime juice
½ cup minced chives
Pickled ginger, cut in fine strips, for garnish

Remove the tendons from the chicken breasts, cut each piece horizontally into 3 slices, and sprinkle with the salt and tellicherry pepper.

Melt 1 tablespoon of the butter in a large nonstick frying pan and brown the chicken pieces, in batches of 4, for about 30 seconds per side. Transfer the chicken to a plate and cover with aluminum foil. Melt another tablespoon of butter and continue until all the chicken pieces are cooked. Add a bit more butter and continue to brown the next batch of 4. (Between batches, remove the burnt butter with paper towels.) When all the chicken pieces are browned, wipe the frying pan with paper towels.

Add the vermouth and boil until reduced to 1 tablespoon. Add the Beef Stock, grated ginger, and lime juice, and cook over moderate heat until the liquid has been reduced by half. Strain the sauce, return it to the pan, and season with additional salt and tellicherry pepper. With the sauce at a simmer, whisk in the remaining tablespoon of butter, turn off the heat, and stir in the minced chives.

Just before serving, return the chicken pieces to the sauce and reheat gently. Arrange the chicken on warm dinner plates, spoon some sauce over each serving, and garnish with ginger strips.

Chicken Breasts
Filled with Goat Cheese and Nasturtium

If your herb market doesn't have nasturtium, try a garden center. The petals make a spectacular edible garnish, as long as they weren't sprayed. Watercress is a good substitute.

Makes 6 servings

3 tablespoons butter, softened
12 nasturtium petals or watercress leaves,
*   6 minced, 6 left whole for garnish*
Pinch of salt
1 tablespoon coarsely ground black
*   pepper*
6 chicken breast halves, skin and bones
*   removed, about 6 ounces each*
3 ounces goat cheese
¼ cup tightly packed nasturtium or
*   watercress leaves*
2 tablespoons olive oil
¼ cup tarragon vinegar

Blend the butter, minced nasturtium petals, salt, and pepper in a mixing bowl. Set aside.

Remove the tenderloins (the finger-size portion) from the chicken breasts and reserve them for another use. Cut away the tendons and remove all visible fat. Make a pocket in each breast half by cutting a horizontal incision in the thickest part. Sprinkle both sides lightly with additional salt to taste.

Purée the goat cheese and the ¼ cup of nasturtium or watercress leaves in the workbowl of a food processor, spread the purée inside the chicken-breast pocket, and secure each piece with a toothpick.

Heat half the olive oil in a nonstick frying pan, and brown half the chicken over moderate heat for 3 minutes per side. Transfer to a plate and cover with aluminum foil. Add the remaining olive oil and repeat with the remaining chicken.

Wipe the frying pan with a paper towel, add the tarragon vinegar, and boil to reduce to about 1 tablespoon. Turn off the heat, and add the reserved nasturtium butter mixture. Swirl the pan until the butter melts.

Remove the toothpicks from the chicken breasts and cut each into 8 parts. Arrange the chicken pieces in crescent pattern in the center of each of 6 large dinner plates, drizzle with the nasturtium-flavored butter, and serve garnished with the whole nasturtium petals or watercress leaves.

Chicken Breasts with Juniper Berries

Juniper berries are usually used as a seasoning for game, so you might not think of pairing them with a meat as mild as chicken. But they work well and add a bold flavor to this dish.

Makes 6 servings

2 tablespoons juniper berries
6 chicken breast halves, skin and bones
    removed, about 6 ounces each
Salt and freshly ground black pepper to
    taste
1 tablespoon gin
4 tablespoons (½ stick) butter plus
    additional for preparing dish and foil
1 medium onion, chopped
1 large carrot, chopped
2 stalks celery, chopped
1 cup dry red wine
2 cups Chicken Stock (page 155)
Lemon juice to taste
Fresh rosemary sprigs, for garnish

Preheat oven to 400°F.

Place the juniper berries in a plastic bag and crush them with a rolling pin or other heavy kitchen tool.

Remove the tendons from the chicken breasts and sprinkle them generously with salt and pepper. Divide the crushed juniper berries among chicken breasts and press the berries into the chicken by pounding lightly with a rolling pin. Drizzle the gin over the chicken pieces.

Heat 1 tablespoon of the butter in a large nonstick frying pan, and brown the chicken breasts in 2 batches over high heat for 1 minute per side. Transfer to an ovenproof dish and add another tablespoon of butter before browning the remaining chicken breasts. Brush a piece of aluminum foil with butter and place the foil, buttered side down, over the chicken breasts. Place in the oven for 10 minutes.

Wipe the frying pan with paper towels and heat the remaining 2 tablespoons of butter. When it's foaming, add the onion and cook over low heat until softened, about 3 minutes. Add the carrot and celery and cook 5 minutes more. Transfer the vegetables to a plate. Add the wine to the pan, turn up the heat, and cook until only 2 tablespoons of wine remain. Add the Chicken Stock and chicken juices from the ovenproof dish, and boil to reduce the sauce to half its original volume. Season with additional salt and pepper and with lemon juice.

Divide the vegetables among 6 dinner plates. Slice the chicken breasts horizontally in half, and place 2 pieces of chicken atop the vegetables on each plate. Spoon the sauce on top, and garnish each serving with a rosemary sprig.

Chicken Breasts
with Mango Chutney and Green Beans

Spice rubs are a wonderful way to transfer flavor to chicken. In order to get the full flavor of the spices, rub the chicken breasts with the spice mixture one hour before cooking.

Makes 6 servings

6 chicken breast halves, skin and bones
removed, about 6 ounces each
Salt to taste
1 tablespoon grated ginger
3 medium cloves garlic, minced
½ teaspoon ground cumin
½ teaspoon ground cinnamon
½ teaspoon ground coriander
½ teaspoon ground turmeric
½ teaspoon ground cloves
¼ teaspoon cayenne pepper
1½ pounds tender, young green beans,
tips removed and rinsed
¼ cup flour
2 tablespoons safflower oil
2 tablespoons butter
3 cups Beef Stock (page 152) or Chicken
Stock (page 155)
¼ cup spicy, shredded mango chutney
(available in Asian food markets)
6 tablespoons crème fraîche (page 157) or
sour cream

Remove the tendons from the chicken breasts and slice each half horizontally into 2 pieces. Sprinkle lightly with salt.

Divide the ginger and garlic evenly over the chicken pieces. Combine the cumin, cinnamon, coriander, turmeric, cloves, and cayenne pepper, and rub the mixture over all surfaces of the chicken. Wrap the chicken with plastic wrap, and refrigerate for 1 hour.

Bring about 4 quarts of salted water to a boil in a large pot, and cook the green beans for 5 to 7 minutes, or until they are tender but still firm. Drain the beans and plunge them into ice water to stop the cooking and set their color, then drain and set aside.

Dredge each piece of chicken in the flour. Heat 1 tablespoon of the oil and 1 tablespoon of the butter in a large frying pan and brown the chicken pieces in batches of 4 over moderate heat for 1 minute per side. Add a bit more oil and butter between batches and, if the butter starts to burn, wipe the pan with paper towels before adding the oil and butter for the next batch.

Add the stock to the pan, reduce its volume by one-third, stir in the chutney, reheat, and adjust salt. Stir in the *crème fraîche.*

Just before serving, gently heat the chicken pieces in the sauce. Place the beans in the center of a serving plate, pile the chicken pieces on top, and spoon the sauce over.

Chicken Breasts
with Peanut Crust and Port Wine

As much as I like flavor contrasts, I also enjoy texture contrasts. Many nuts go beautifully with chicken. I like peanuts for this recipe. Their crunch contrasts well with the soft, tender chicken, and the broiling permeates the kitchen with the aroma of freshly roasted peanuts. The drawback is that peanuts burn easily, so to avoid a fiasco, pay close attention to the broiling process.

Makes 6 servings

6 chicken breast halves, skin and bones
removed, about 6 ounces each
Salt to taste
½ teaspoon freshly ground black pepper
4 tablespoons (½ stick) butter
½ cup Port wine
2 cups Chicken Stock (page 155)
Lemon juice to taste
1 tablespoon cornstarch mixed with 2
tablespoons water
6 small clusters seedless white grapes,
rinsed, for garnish
6 tablespoons unsalted red-skinned
peanuts, chopped

Remove the tendons from the chicken breasts and cut each piece in half horizontally. Season with the salt and black pepper.

Melt 2 tablespoons of the butter in a large nonstick frying pan and brown the chicken pieces in batches of 4 for 1 minute per side. Place the browned chicken in a roasting pan large enough to hold the pieces in a single layer and cover with aluminum foil. Wipe the frying pan with paper towels, add more butter, and repeat with remaining chicken slices.

Add the wine to the pan, and boil to reduce the volume to 3 tablespoons. Add the stock, boil for 5 minutes, season with additional salt and pepper and with the lemon juice, stir in the cornstarch mixture, and simmer until the sauce has lightly thickened. Add the grape clusters to the sauce to warm them.

Sprinkle the chopped peanuts over the chicken. Set an oven rack on the second position from the top, preheat the broiler, and broil the chicken breasts for 30 seconds or until the peanut crust is golden brown.

Spoon some sauce onto each of 6 dinner plates, place 2 chicken pieces in the center of each plate, and garnish each plate with a grape cluster.

Chicken Breasts Wrapped in Poblano Chilies

Poblano chilies have a smoky and piquant flavor. This Mexican-style dish can be prepared hours before guests arrive because the thick-fleshed poblano wrapping and the sauce keep the chicken moist. The chocolate is used here to make the sauce smooth, not sweet. Chipotle chilies have a smoky flavor.

Makes 6 servings

6 chicken breast halves, skin and bones
    removed, about 6 ounces each
Salt to taste
2 tablespoons chili powder
¼ cup olive oil
12 poblano chilies or 6 yellow bell
    peppers, roasted (page 161)
1 medium onion, minced
2 cloves garlic, minced
1 tablespoon ground cumin
1 canned chipotle chili in adobe sauce,
    drained, seeded and minced
2 cups Chicken Stock (page 155) or
    canned chicken broth
1 ounce bittersweet chocolate
12 slices Monterey Jack cheese, each cut
    to ½ inch by 3 inches
6 tablespoons minced cilantro, for
    garnish

Remove the tendons from the chicken breasts, and cut each piece in half horizontally. Sprinkle lightly with salt, and rub the chili powder over all surfaces of the chicken.

Heat 1 tablespoon of the olive oil in a nonstick frying pan, and brown the chicken pieces, in batches of 4 for 1 minute per side. Add another 1 tablespoon of olive oil before each batch. Wrap each piece of chicken with a poblano chili or half a bell pepper, and arrange in a single layer in an ovenproof baking dish.

Preheat oven to 400°F.

Add the remaining 1 tablespoon of olive oil to the frying pan, and cook the onion and garlic over low heat until they are softened. Sprinkle with cumin, increase the heat, add the chipotle, stock, and chocolate, and stir until the chocolate has melted. Simmer for 2 minutes, season with additional salt to taste, and pour sauce over the wrapped chicken. Top with the cheese slices. (The recipe can be prepared ahead to this point.)

Just before serving, place the pan in the oven and bake for 10 minutes. Serve garnished with chopped cilantro.

Chicken Breasts
with Vegetables and Champagne Sauce

Many recipes—this one, for example—have low-calorie alternates. You could poach the chicken instead of frying it, and you could omit the *crème fraîche,* confident that the vegetables will carry the dish nicely.

Makes 6 servings

2 cups Chicken Stock (page 155)
1 cup dry champagne
2 carrots, peeled and cut in julienne
1 celery root, cut in julienne
1 large leek (see note)
6 chicken breast halves, skin and bones
    removed, about 6 ounces each
Salt and freshly ground black pepper to
    taste
4 tablespoons (½ stick) butter
1 tablespoon cornstarch mixed with
    2 tablespoons cold water
Romaine lettuce leaves, rinsed and dried,
    for garnish
¾ cup crème fraîche (page 157) or
    whipped cream

Combine the Chicken Stock and champagne in a large pot, and boil for 10 minutes. Add the carrots and celery root and simmer for 3 minutes; add the leek and simmer for 1 minute more. With a slotted spoon, transfer the vegetables to an ovenproof dish. Reserve the liquid.

Preheat oven to 400°F.

Remove the tendons from the chicken breasts, and sprinkle the meat with salt and pepper. Melt 2 tablespoons of the butter in a large nonstick frying pan. When the butter is foaming, brown half the chicken pieces for 1 minute per side. Place the browned chicken on top of the vegetables. Add the remaining 2 tablespoons of butter to the pan, brown the remaining chicken breasts, and add them to the baking dish. Cover the dish with aluminum foil and place in the oven for 5 minutes. Remove promptly.

Place the cooking liquid from the vegetables and any pan drippings over high heat and reduce to half its original volume. Whisk in the cornstarch mixture, simmer until the sauce has lightly thickened, and season to taste with additional salt and pepper. (This dish can be prepared ahead to this point.)

Stack and roll the lettuce leaves, then cut them into fine shreds.

Just before serving, bring the sauce to a boil, whisk in the *crème fraîche*, and turn off the heat. Divide the vegetables among 6 dinner plates, and set a chicken breast on top. Ladle some of the sauce over the chicken, and garnish with shredded lettuce leaves.

Note: To prepare the leek, cut off the roots, remove the tough outer leaves, and trim the tops, leaving 5 inches of the green part. Cut in half lengthwise and rinse thoroughly under cold running water, spreading the leaves to rinse off soil lodged in between. Cut crosswise into ½-inch pieces.

Chicken Fingers with Cucumber and Dill

Chicken fingers are the part of the chicken breast sometimes sold as "tenders," "breast filets," or "chicken stir-fry." It can be tedious to remove the tendons from such small pieces, so if time is of the essence, use whole chicken breasts instead.

Makes 6 servings

2½ pounds chicken fingers, about 30 pieces
Salt and freshly ground black pepper to taste
3 tablespoons canola oil
2 tablespoons butter plus additional to prepare foil
⅓ cup rice wine vinegar
⅓ cup dry white wine
3 shallots, minced
2 cups Chicken Stock (page 155)
1 tablespoon cornstarch mixed with 2 tablespoons water
1 large seedless cucumber, about 1 pound
½ teaspoon salt
½ cup fresh dill, minced
Dill sprigs, for garnish

Set an oven rack on the middle position and preheat the oven to 325°F.

Remove the tendons from the chicken fingers and sprinkle the pieces with salt and pepper. Divide them into 3 batches. Heat 1 tablespoon of the oil in a large nonstick frying pan, and brown the first batch of the chicken fingers over high heat for 2 minutes. Transfer them to a baking pan, add 1 more tablespoon of oil to the frying pan, and repeat with the second batch. Repeat with the third batch. Butter a piece of aluminum foil and place it, buttered side down, over the browned chicken fingers. Bake in the oven for 15 minutes and remove promptly.

In a small saucepan, combine the vinegar, wine, and shallots, and cook until the liquid has evaporated. Add the Chicken Stock and boil to reduce the liquid by half. Stir in the cornstarch mixture to thicken lightly, season to taste with additional salt and pepper, and add any pan drippings released while baking the chicken fingers.

Peel the cucumber and cut it in half lengthwise. Scrape out the soft center and slice into ¼-inch-thick half-moons. Heat 2 tablespoons of butter in same frying pan used to brown the chicken fingers, and, when it's foamy, add the sliced cucumber, salt, and additional freshly ground black pepper to taste. Stir-fry over moderate to high heat for 3 minutes, add the minced dill, and remove the pan from the heat.

Divide the cucumbers pieces among 6 dinner plates, placing them in the center of each. Place a portion of the chicken fingers on top, and cover with sauce. Garnish with dill sprigs.

Chicken Fingers with Lingonberry Sauce

Lingonberries have an interesting taste because of their unusual flavor combination—sweet and tart. They grow wild in northern Sweden and Norway.

Makes 6 servings

4 tablespoons (½ stick) butter
6 tablespoons Dijon mustard
2 ½ pounds chicken fingers, about 30 pieces
Salt and freshly ground black pepper
4 carrots, cut in julienne strips
½ cup water
2 tablespoons lemon juice
½ teaspoon grated lemon rind
¼ cup Madeira wine
2 cups Beef Stock (page 152) or Chicken Stock (page 155) (see note)
½ cup lingonberries in syrup, drained (available in specialty stores)
½ teaspoon ground cinnamon

Melt the butter, and whisk in the mustard until smooth. Remove the tendons from the chicken fingers and pat dry with paper towels, and place them in a single layer into a large baking pan. Sprinkle with salt and pepper, coat with the mustard-butter mixture, and refrigerate for 1 hour.

Place the carrots, water, lemon juice, lemon rind, and a pinch of salt into a medium saucepan and simmer, covered, for 5 minutes. Set aside.

Preheat the broiler to high and set the oven rack 7 inches from the broiler. Broil the chicken fingers for 5 minutes, transfer to a plate, and cover with aluminum foil. Pour the Madeira into the baking pan and scrape up any baked-on juices. Strain the juices into a saucepan, add the stock, lingonberries, and cinnamon, and boil until the liquid has been reduced by half. Season to taste with additional salt and freshly ground black pepper.

To serve, heap about 5 chicken fingers in the center of each of 6 warm dinner plates. Add any accumulated juices from the chicken fingers to the sauce and reheat gently. Divide the sauce over the chicken fingers, drain the carrots, and place them on top.

Note: Although either stock works here, Beef Stock has more body and would be better.

Chicken Thighs with Fragrant Vegetables

Chicken thighs lend themselves to longer-cooking methods, and that can infuse the meat with great flavors. Here, the sharp, sweet-sour taste of the tamarind is where the most flavor comes from.

Makes 6 servings

4 fresh plum tomatoes, cut into small cubes
2 cloves garlic, minced
1 cup basil leaves, chopped
1 tablespoon grated lemon zest
2 large leeks, tough outer leaves removed
    and trimmed
2 carrots, peeled and diced
18 chicken thighs, about 6 pounds before
    trimming, skin, bones, and extra fat
    removed
1 teaspoon salt
1 teaspoon freshly ground black pepper
¼ cup flour
¼ cup olive oil
1 large onion, cut into ¼-inch-thick rings

Flavored stock:
4 cups canned chicken broth
10 thin slices fresh, peeled gingerroot
1 tablespoon tamarind concentrate
    (available in Asian markets)
8 allspice berries

Preheat oven to 325°F. Combine the tomatoes, garlic, basil, and lemon rind. Set aside.

Make the flavored stock by combining the chicken broth, ginger, tamarind, and allspice, and boil for 15 minutes. Strain and set aside.

While the stock is boiling, cut off and discard the roots and half of the green part of the leeks. Slice in half lengthwise. To remove soil lodged between individual leaves, spread them apart while rinsing under cold running water. Cut crosswise into ½-inch pieces. Combine with the diced carrots and set aside.

Sprinkle the chicken thighs with salt and pepper, then dredge the pieces in the flour. On the stovetop, heat 2 tablespoons of the olive oil in a Dutch oven until very hot, and brown the chicken thighs in batches of 5 or 6 on both sides. Transfer the browned chicken thighs to a plate, add more of the olive oil and repeat with the second batch. Repeat until all the chicken is browned. Wipe the Dutch oven with paper towels, add 1 tablespoon of the olive oil, and cook the onion rings over low heat until they are soft.

Add the flavored chicken broth and bring to a boil. Add carrots and leeks, simmer for 3 minutes, remove the vegetables with a slotted spoon, and set them aside. Return the chicken thighs to the Dutch oven, cover, and cook in the oven for 30 minutes.

Add additional salt and freshly ground black pepper to taste, and stir in the vegetables and the tomato mixture. Turn off the heat and let stand for 5 minutes before serving.

Chicken Thighs with Red Wine Sauce

Don't be discouraged by the long list of ingredients. The marinade takes only 5 minutes to prepare and the actual cooking time is only 30 minutes, most of it untended. It can be prepared ahead of time and your guests will be delighted by its presentation.

Makes 6 servings

*18 chicken thighs, about 6 pounds before
    trimming, skin, bones, and extra fat
    removed*
*1 whole onion, unpeeled, with 1 bay leaf
    attached with 2 whole cloves*
1 sprig fresh rosemary or 1 teaspoon dried
12 whole juniper berries
1 stalk celery, chopped
1 carrot, peeled and chopped
*1 leek, cut in half lengthwise, rinsed and
    chopped*
*3 cups full-bodied dry red wine, such as
    Chianti or Burgundy*
¼ cup vegetable oil
1 teaspoon salt
1 teaspoon freshly ground black pepper
Flour, for dredging
*3 cloves garlic, mashed through a garlic
    press*
2 cups canned chicken broth

Garnish:
*8 ½-inch-thick slices French bread
    (baguette)*
3 tablespoons butter, melted
4 strips bacon
*1 jar (6 ounces) small white pickled onions,
    drained*

Place the chicken thighs in a large bowl with the onion, rosemary, juniper berries, celery, carrot, and leek. Pour the wine over the mixture, cover, and refrigerate for 48 hours. Stir every 12 hours. Remove the chicken from the marinade and dry each piece thoroughly with paper towels. Strain the marinade and save 1 cup.

Preheat oven to 350°F.

On the stovetop, heat 2 tablespoons of the oil in a large Dutch oven. Sprinkle the thighs with salt and pepper, dredge each piece in the flour, and brown the chicken, on both sides, in batches of 4 or 5 over high heat. Add more oil before browning the second and third batches. Set the chicken aside. Add the garlic to the Dutch oven and cook over low heat for 2 minutes while scraping bottom of pan. Add the reserved marinade and the Chicken Stock, bring to a boil, return the chicken to the sauce, cover, and bake for 30 minutes. Remove from oven.

Brush the bread slices on both sides with the melted butter and place them on a cookie sheet. Toast the bread for 10 minutes in the oven, cool on a rack, and cut into small croutons. While the croutons cool, brown the bacon strips until crisp. Crumble the bacon and set aside. Discard all but 2 tablespoons of the bacon fat and brown the small white onions in the fat. (The recipe can be prepared in advance to this point.)

Just before serving, reheat the chicken thighs on top of the stove. Divide the chicken thighs among 6 preheated dinner plates, spoon the sauce on top, and sprinkle each serving with bacon, onions, and croutons.

Chicken Thighs with Two Paprikas

Forget the notion that paprika does nothing but add a little color. Authentic Hungarian paprika gives this dish a vibrant color, but a blend of sweet and hot paprika adds a slight bite without overwhelming the flavor of the chicken.

Makes 6 servings

2 yellow bell peppers, roasted (page 161) and cut into strips
1 tablespoon lemon juice
Salt and freshly ground black pepper to taste
18 chicken thighs, about 6 pounds before trimming, skin, bones, and extra fat removed
¼ cup sweet paprika (Szeged brand)
¼ teaspoon hot paprika (Szeged brand)
1 teaspoon salt
5 tablespoons olive oil, approximately
¼ cup flour
1 small onion, minced
3 large cloves garlic, minced
½ cup dry white wine
3 cups canned chicken or beef broth

Combine the strips of roasted pepper with the lemon juice, salt, and black pepper. Set aside.

Place the chicken thighs in a mixing bowl. Blend the two paprika powders with the 1 teaspoon of salt, and rub chicken thighs with the mixture.

Preheat oven to 325°F.

Heat 2 tablespoons of the olive oil in a Dutch oven on the stovetop. Dredge the chicken thighs in the flour, then brown the thighs on both sides in batches of 4 or 5 over moderate heat. Transfer the browned thighs to a plate, wipe the pan, and repeat with remaining chicken thighs, adding more oil before each batch. You'll have used about ¼ cup of oil.

Wipe the Dutch oven with paper towels and heat the remaining 1 tablespoon of the olive oil. Over low heat, cook but do not brown the onion and garlic until soft. Add the wine, turn up the heat and reduce the wine to 2 tablespoons, add the chicken broth, return the chicken thighs to the sauce, cover, and bake in the oven for 30 minutes.

Arrange the chicken thighs among 6 dinner plates, spoon some sauce on top of each serving, and place the pepper strips in a grid pattern on top.

Chicken Thighs with Yellow Lentils and Cilantro

Lentils are so hearty that by combining them with chicken you can stretch the number of servings you'll get from this recipe.

Makes 6 to 8 servings

1 cup yellow lentils
4 cups water
1 tablespoon salt
18 chicken thighs, about 6 pounds before trimming, skin, bones, and extra fat removed
1 teaspoon salt
1 teaspoon freshly ground black pepper
¼ cup flour
3 tablespoons olive oil, approximately
1 large onion, cut into rings
4 cloves garlic, minced
6 ounces canned crushed tomatoes
3 cups canned chicken or beef broth
2 cups cilantro leaves, rinsed, dried, and chopped
1 large clove garlic, put through a garlic press
1 tablespoon lemon juice

Preheat oven to 350°F.

Remove any debris from the lentils and thoroughly rinse them. Bring water and salt to a boil, cook the lentils for 2 minutes, drain, and set aside.

Sprinkle the chicken thighs with the salt and pepper and dredge each piece in the flour. Heat 2 tablespoons of the olive oil in a Dutch oven on the stovetop, and brown the chicken thighs on both sides, in batches of 4 or 5, over high heat. Transfer the browned chicken thighs to a plate. Repeat with remaining chicken thighs, adding a bit more olive oil before browning each batch.

Add 1 tablespoon olive oil to the Dutch oven, and cook the onion rings and minced garlic, covered, for 5 minutes over low heat. Return the chicken thighs to the Dutch oven, add the crushed tomatoes, broth, and cooked lentils to the chicken, cover, and place in the oven for 30 minutes. (The recipe can be prepared ahead to this point.)

Just before serving, combine the cilantro, mashed garlic, and lemon juice. Divide the chicken-lentil dish among 6 dinner plates, and serve garnished with the cilantro mixture.

Cold Chicken Breasts with Cantaloupe and Fresh Mint

The main ingredients and garnishes combine for a very colorful dish that's ideal for a summer lunch or as part of a buffet table.

Makes 6 to 8 servings

4 cups Chicken Stock (page 155) or canned chicken broth
6 chicken breast halves, skin and bones removed, about 6 ounces each
1 extra-large egg
2 extra-large egg yolks
¾ cup safflower oil
2 tablespoons curry powder (Madras brand)
Pinch of sugar
3 tablespoons lemon juice
1 tablespoon Dijon mustard
1 cup fresh mint leaves, rinsed and dried
Salt to taste
1 cantaloupe, well-ripened but still firm
Mint sprigs, for garnish

Bring the stock to a boil, add the chicken breasts, simmer for 4 minutes, turn the chicken, and simmer for 4 minutes more. The chicken should be submerged for all the cooking. Transfer the chicken to a plate, sprinkle it with a bit of the liquid, cover with clear plastic wrap, and refrigerate. Strain the stock, reserve ¼ cup, and freeze the rest for future use.

Place the egg and the 2 yolks in the workbowl of a food processor and mix briefly. With the machine running, add the oil in a thin stream to make a mayonnaise. Add the curry powder, sugar, lemon juice, mustard, and mint, and process until the mint leaves are finely chopped. Add the ¼ cup of reserved Chicken Stock, add salt and additional lemon juice to taste, and refrigerate. (The recipe can be prepared in advance to this point.)

Just before serving, cut each chicken piece horizontally into 3 slices.

Wash the outside of the cantaloupe. Cut the melon in half, remove the seeds, and cut into wedges, each about ⅛ inch thick. Cut away the rind and place the melon wedges, alternating with the chicken slices on a serving dish. For individual servings, use a special blade of the food processor to slice the cantaloupe paper-thin. Pile the slices in the center of each plate, and fan 3 chicken slices on top. Regardless of how you serve it, spoon some dressing on top, garnish with mint sprigs, and pass the remaining dressing at the table.

Cold Chicken Breasts with Honey and Star Anise

Star anise is one of the most fragrant spices and is used in many Asian dishes. Its dense, licorice flavor lends this dish an exotic aroma.

Makes 6 servings

6 chicken breast halves, skin and bones removed, about 6 ounces each

Marinade:
½ cup soy sauce
1 cup water
1 cup canned chicken broth
¾ cup honey
1 teaspoon ground allspice
3 whole star anise
2 tablespoons ginger, finely grated
3 cloves garlic, finely grated

Dressing:
1 extra-large egg
2 extra-large egg yolks
½ cup safflower oil
2 tablespoons dark sesame oil
2 tablespoons rice vinegar
1 tablespoon lime juice
3 drops Tabasco sauce
1 tablespoon soy sauce

Garnish:
¼ pound snow peas, ends removed
2 tablespoons roasted sesame seeds

Pound the chicken breasts lightly with a rolling pin between sheets of wax paper until they are of even thickness.

Make the marinade by combining the ½ cup of soy sauce, water, broth, honey, allspice, star anise, ginger, and garlic in a large saucepan and bring to a boil. Reduce the heat, add the chicken breasts, and cook, with the liquid barely simmering, for 4 minutes, being sure that the breasts are submerged for the entire cooking time. Turn the chicken, and simmer for 4 minutes more. Transfer the chicken to a plate, and cover. Strain and reserve ¼ cup of the marinade.

Make the dressing by placing the whole egg and the 2 yolks in the workbowl of a food processor. Mix briefly and add the safflower oil in a thin stream to make a mayonnaise. Blend in the sesame oil, rice vinegar, lime juice, Tabasco, soy sauce, and the reserved marinade.

Bring about 2 quarts of salted water to the boil. Place the snow peas in the water, remove the pot from the heat, cover, and, after 3 minutes, drain the peas and plunge them into ice water to set their color.

Cut each chicken breast horizontally into 3 slices. Fan the chicken slices and alternate them with the snow peas in the center of individual dinner plates, spoon the dressing on top, and sprinkle each serving with the sesame seeds.

Cold Chicken Breasts with Lemon and Caper Dressing

Capers are unopened, pickled flower buds from the caper bush. You can buy several varieties and sizes. The firm, small nonpareil from France used in this recipe add flavor as well as texture.

Makes 6 servings

6 chicken breast halves, skin and bones removed, about 6 ounces each
Salt and freshly ground black pepper to taste
4 cups Chicken Stock (page 155) or canned chicken broth
12 medium cloves garlic, peeled
1 tablespoon black peppercorns
Zest of 1 lemon, cut into julienne
1 extra-large egg
2 extra-large egg yolks
¾ cup safflower oil
1 tablespoon Dijon mustard
Pinch of sugar
1 tablespoon lemon juice
¼ cup nonpareil capers, drained

Sprinkle the chicken breasts lightly with salt and pepper, place the pieces between sheets of wax paper, and pound lightly to an even thickness.

Bring the stock, garlic, and peppercorns to a boil, lower the heat, and simmer for 30 minutes. Poach the chicken breasts, which should be fully submerged, for 4 minutes, then turn them and cook for 4 minutes more. Transfer the chicken to a plate, spoon a bit of stock over the pieces, cover with clear plastic, and refrigerate. Strain the stock, reserve ¼ cup, and freeze the rest for later use.

Bring about 1 cup of water to a boil and simmer the lemon zest for 1 minute. Drain and place on a paper towel.

Place the egg and the egg yolks into the workbowl of a food processor. Blend briefly and add the oil in a thin stream to make a mayonnaise. Blend in the mustard, sugar, lemon juice, reserved Chicken Stock, and additional salt and pepper to taste. Refrigerate. (This recipe can be prepared in advance to this point.)

Just before serving, slice each chicken breast horizontally into 3 or 4 slices. Arrange the slices on each of 6 dinner plates, spoon some dressing on top, and sprinkle each dish with capers and lemon zest. Pass remaining dressing at the table.

Cold Chicken Breasts with Oranges and a Green Dressing

A homemade mayonnaise is a wonderful way to dress up a dish. This version uses only egg whites, so it's more healthful than most. The orange extract and orange juice concentrate give it an assertive flavor.

Makes 6 servings

6 chicken breast halves, skin and bones removed, about 6 ounces each
Salt and freshly ground black pepper to taste
4 cups Chicken Stock (page 155) or canned chicken broth
½ cup dry white wine
1 pound green beans, tips removed
3 extra-large egg whites
Pinch of cream of tartar
¾ cup canola oil
1 cup tightly packed watercress leaves, tough stems removed, rinsed, and dried
¼ cup frozen orange-juice concentrate
½ teaspoon orange extract
1 tablespoon Dijon mustard
1 tablespoon cider vinegar
4 large navel oranges, cut into segments (see note)

Sprinkle the chicken breasts lightly with salt and pepper, cover them with wax paper, and pound them to an even thickness.

Bring the stock and wine to a boil in a large pot, simmer for 5 minutes, and add the chicken breasts, 3 pieces at a time. Simmer for 4 minutes, turn chicken, and simmer for 4 more minutes. Transfer the chicken to a plate, sprinkle a bit of stock over the chicken, cover, and refrigerate. Strain the stock and store in the freezer for future use.

Rinse the pot, add about 4 quarts of water with 2 tablespoons of salt, bring to the boil, and cook the green beans for 4 minutes, or until they are tender but still firm. Drain the beans, rinse with ice-cold water, and set aside.

Place the egg whites in the workbowl of a food processor, add the cream of tartar, and process for 10 seconds. With the machine running, add the oil in a thin stream to make a mayonnaise. Add the watercress leaves, and process for 30 seconds. Blend in the orange-juice concentrate, orange extract, mustard, and vinegar. Season to taste with additional salt and pepper.

Cut the chicken breasts horizontally into thin slices, arrange them on a large serving platter, top with the dressing, and place the green beans, in bundles of 5, on top of each chicken piece. Garnish with the orange segments.

Note: With a bit of practice, cutting oranges into segments is quite simple. Make a cut into the orange, slicing very close to the membrane of one segment. At the center of the orange, twist the knife so the segment will lift out. Repeat all the way around the orange. Or, cut the orange into ¼-inch thick slices and cut away the peel and white pith.

Cold Chicken Breasts
with Szechuan Peppercorns and Pancakes

Everything you need for this recipe can be made in advance, making it a great dish for a dinner party. Just be careful not to over-marinate the chicken.

Makes 6 servings

½ cup soy sauce
¼ cup rice vinegar
2 tablespoons lemon juice
¼ cup honey
¼ cup safflower oil, approximately
½ teaspoon chili oil
2 tablespoons Szechuan peppercorns
Flour Pancakes (recipe follows)
6 chicken breast halves, skin and bones
*   removed, about 6 ounces each*
4 carrots, cut into julienne strips
1 can (8 ounces) shredded bamboo
*   shoots, drained, rinsed, and dried*

Combine the soy sauce, rice vinegar, lemon juice, honey, 2 tablespoons of the safflower oil, the chili oil, and the Szechuan peppercorns, and refrigerate for 4 hours or overnight. This will be the marinade. Strain through a sieve before using.

Prepare the pancakes using the recipe that follows. They can be prepared up to 3 days ahead.

Slice the chicken breasts horizontally into 3 pieces. Brush a nonstick frying pan

with 1 tablespoon of the remaining safflower oil, and brown the chicken pieces, in batches of 5 or 6, over high heat for 1 minute on each side. Add a bit more oil before browning the second batch. Repeat for the third batch. Place the browned chicken pieces on a cutting board and cut into ½-inch-thick strips. Place the strips in a mixing bowl.

Using the same frying pan, stir-fry the carrots and bamboo shoots over high heat for 3 minutes and add to the chicken. One hour before serving, pour the marinade over the chicken strips, carrots, and bamboo shoots, and blend well. Keep at room temperature.

Preheat oven to 325°F, and place the wrapped pancakes in the oven for 10 minutes.

Remove the chicken pieces from the marinade, drain the vegetables, and save the marinade as a dipping sauce. Arrange the chicken and vegetables on a serving dish and serve the warm pancakes separately.

Demonstrate to your guests how to assemble this dish. Spoon a generous amount of chicken and vegetables into the center of a pancake, bring up the lower part of the pancake to cover the chicken, fold in the two sides, and roll up.

Flour Pancakes

Makes 6 double-pancakes

1 ½ cups flour
¾ cup boiling water
¼ cup sesame oil, approximately

Place the flour in a mixing bowl and slowly add the boiling water while mixing with a fork. Place the dough on a lightly floured surface and knead for 5 minutes until smooth. Cover the dough with a damp towel, and set aside for 30 minutes.

Place the dough on a lightly floured surface and, with floured hands, shape into a 12-inch long cylinder. Divide into 12 even portions and roll each portion into a round about 4 inches in diameter.

Brush the first pancake lightly with sesame oil and place a second pancake on top. Press together with rolling pin and roll them out until they measure 9 inches in diameter. Repeat to make 6 double pancakes.

Heat a nonstick frying pan over medium heat and brush the pan with sesame oil. Add one of the double pancakes and cook for 1 minute on each side. Transfer to a plate and, while still hot, pull them apart into 2 single pancakes. Continue with remaining pancakes, brushing the pan with additional oil if necessary. Wrap the pancakes with aluminum foil and refrigerate.

Use as directed in previous recipe.

Smoked Turkey Breast
with Grapes and Horseradish Dressing

If you need something really fast, this is it. This recipe requires only half a smoked turkey breast, but if you must buy a whole breast from your poultry purveyor, freeze the extra half.

Makes 8 to 10 servings

3 extra-large egg yolks
¾ cup canola oil
2 tablespoons Dijon mustard
3 tablespoons cider vinegar
Pinch of sugar
3 drops Tabasco sauce
¼ teaspoon salt
6 ounces prepared storebought
　　horseradish
½ cup slivered blanched almonds
1 smoked turkey breast half, 3 to 4
　　pounds before trimming, skin, bones,
　　and fat removed, cut in thin slices
½ pound white seedless grapes, rinsed
　　and cut in small clusters
½ pound black seedless grapes, rinsed
　　and cut in small clusters

Make a mayonnaise by processing the egg yolks in the workbowl of a food processor and, with the machine running, slowly adding the oil in a thin stream. Add the mustard, vinegar, sugar, Tabasco, salt, and horseradish, blend, transfer to a bowl, and refrigerate.

Toast the almonds in a large nonstick frying pan over low heat, stirring frequently until they are golden brown. Transfer to paper towels.

Arrange the turkey slices on a serving plate. Partially cover the slices with the dressing, sprinkle with the toasted almonds, and garnish with the grape clusters.

Duck Breasts

Duck breasts are often sold in packages of two whole breasts, with a total weight of about 1½ pounds. Half a breast per person is sufficient if you also serve a first course. Remove duck breasts from the refrigerator one hour before cooking. Two methods are used. Begin roasting with the skin side up, which keeps the meat moist. Then fry the breasts just before serving to give the skin a crisp, golden finish. Serve with any sauce from the poultry section.

Makes 6 servings

**8 duck breast halves, (Peking Long
    Island-style) about 5 ounces each,
    with skin, tendon removed
Salt and freshly ground black pepper to
    taste**

Preheat oven to 325°F.

Place the duck breasts, skin side up, in a single layer in a large rectangular roasting pan. Score the skin in a criss-cross pattern without cutting into the meat, and sprinkle both sides lightly with salt and pepper. Roast the breasts for 20 minutes, remove from the oven, transfer to a plate, and cover.

Just before serving, preheat a large cast-iron frying pan on the stovetop. Brown the breast pieces 4 at a time, skin side down, until the skin is crisp and golden. Press down on the breasts with a spatula to squeeze out excess fat. Place the breasts, skin side up, on a carving board and repeat with the remaining breasts. (Or use two frying pans and do both batches simultaneously.) Cut diagonally into slices and, to keep the skin crisp, serve them on top of the sauce.

Duck Breasts with Apples and Cider Sauce

Duck fat is both a curse and a blessing. It keeps the meat from drying, but it's so plentiful that proper cooking requires some way to drain it. That's why it's cooked here in stages. I used the Peking duck (Long Island-style) for this recipe.

Makes 4 servings

2 cups apple cider
2 tablespoons Port wine
1 bay leaf
2 cloves
4 black peppercorns
1 cinnamon stick
2 large Winesap or other tart apples
2 cups Beef Stock (page 152) or Chicken
*   Stock (page 155)*
Salt and freshly ground black pepper to
*   taste*
6 duck breast halves, about 5 ounces
*   each, with skin, tendon removed*
2 tablespoons butter

Combine the cider, wine, bay leaf, cloves, peppercorns, and cinnamon stick in large pot. Bring to a boil, then reduce to a simmer. Meanwhile, peel and core the apples and slice each into 4 rings. Place them into the cider mixture and simmer for 2 minutes. Remove the apples and boil the cider until it's reduced to 1 cup. Strain, return to saucepan, add the stock, and boil until lightly thickened. Season with salt and pepper.

Preheat oven to 325°F.

Trim any loose fat from the duck breasts and remove tendons. Place the breasts skin side up in a heavy-gauge roasting pan large enough to fit the pieces in a single layer. Score the skin in a criss-cross pattern without cutting into the meat, and season both sides lightly with additional salt and freshly ground black pepper. Roast the duck breasts for 20 minutes, transfer them to a cutting board, and cover with aluminum foil.

Melt 1 tablespoon of the butter in a large nonstick frying pan and brown 4 of the apple rings on both sides. Repeat with remaining butter and apple rings.

Just before serving, heat a cast-iron (not enameled) skillet on the stovetop until it's very hot and smoking. Place 3 of the duck pieces, skin side down, in the pan and brown them while pressing down with a spatula to remove excess fat. When the skin is crisp and golden brown, transfer the breasts, skin side up, to a cutting board. Do not cover them. Brown the other 3 pieces. (Or use 2 frying pans and brown the batches simultaneously.) Cut the meat diagonally into ½-inch slices.

Reheat the sauce, spoon a generous amount on each of 4 preheated dinner plates. Arrange 2 apple rings on each plate, and top them with a portion of the duck slices. Serve immediately.

Grilled Chicken Breasts with Kumquats

This is my version of Duck a l'Orange—not as rich but with much less fat!

Makes 6 servings

6 chicken breast halves, skin and bones removed, about 6 ounces each
3 tablespoons olive oil
Salt to taste
2 teaspoons freshly ground tellicherry pepper
1 cup balsamic vinegar
2 cups Chicken Stock (page 155)
6 kumquats (packed in syrup), cut in half, seeded and chopped, plus 3 tablespoons syrup
2 tablespoons butter, in 4 pieces
Watercress, for garnish

Remove the tendons from the chicken breasts and cut each piece in half horizontally. Brush both sides with the olive oil and sprinkle with salt and pepper.

Heat a cast-iron ridged skillet (not enameled) on the stovetop. When the pan is very hot, add the chicken pieces a few at a time, brown for 1 minute, rotate each piece 180 degrees to make a grid pattern, and grill for 2 more minutes. Flip the chicken pieces, and repeat on other side. Transfer to a plate and cover with foil. Repeat with remaining chicken.

Pour the balsamic vinegar into an enameled frying pan and boil until the volume is reduced to 2 tablespoons. Add the Chicken Stock and reduce the volume to about 1 cup. Bring the sauce to a simmer. Add the chopped kumquats and the syrup, adjust salt and pepper, and swirl in the butter a piece at a time. Return the chicken breasts to the sauce and reheat gently.

Arrange the chicken on serving plates, spoon the sauce on top, dividing the kumquat pieces evenly, and garnish with watercress.

Grilled Chicken Breasts with Tomatillos

Chicken's versatility shows itself again here in combination with some very assertive flavors. But it's important to balance those flavors. Hence, I combine the Mexican spices with the cool, tart flavor of the tomatillos.

Makes 6 servings

6 chicken breast halves, skin and bones removed, about 6 ounces each
Salt and freshly ground black pepper to taste
¼ cup olive oil
1½ pounds very ripe tomatoes, skinned, halved, and seeded
½ cup olives, Cerignola or Niçoise, plus 6 for garnish, rinsed and pitted
2 cloves garlic
1 tablespoon anchovy paste
½ pound tomatillos, papery husks removed, or 1 cup canned Mexican green tomatoes, rinsed
½ teaspoon Tabasco sauce
½ teaspoon ground cumin
2 bunches fresh cilantro, rinsed and dried
12 5-inch corn tortillas (storebought)

Remove the tendons from the chicken breasts, cut each piece horizontally in half, and sprinkle lightly with salt and pepper. Drizzle with the olive oil, cover, and refrigerate for 1 hour.

To make the sauce, place the tomato halves in the workbowl of a food processor with the pitted olives, garlic, anchovy paste, tomatillos, Tabasco, and cumin. Process until smooth, and season to taste with additional salt and pepper.

Preheat the oven to 350°F. Wrap the tortillas in aluminum foil and warm in the oven for 15 minutes.

Heat a ridged cast-iron skillet until it's very hot. Grill the chicken pieces in 4 batches for 1 minute, rotate each piece by 180 degrees to make a grid pattern, and grill for 2 more minutes. Flip the chicken pieces and repeat on other side. Transfer chicken to a cutting board, cover with foil, and repeat with the remaining chicken breasts.

Just before serving, cut the chicken breasts into ½-inch strips. Place a handful of cilantro leaves on a serving plate, spoon some of the sauce over the leaves, place the chicken strips on top, and spread remaining sauce over the chicken. Serve at room temperature, garnished with the olives and accompanied with the warm tortillas.

Turkey Chops with Balsamic Vinegar

Balsamic vinegar is an amazing ingredient. In this recipe, it makes the sauce more like a dressing, and by using the same pan there is less cleaning up. After the initial browning, the turkey chops finish cooking in the oven while you prepare the sauce.

Makes 6 servings

2 tablespoons olive oil, more if needed
6 turkey chops, each about 6 ounces and
    1 inch thick
6 cloves garlic, peeled
1 teaspoon salt
1 teaspoon freshly ground black pepper
¼ cup aged balsamic vinegar
2 tablespoons honey
1 tablespoon Dijon mustard
1 cup Beef Stock (page 152) or canned
    beef broth
4 tablespoons (½ stick) butter, cut in
    pieces
6 cups frisée or baby green salad, rinsed
    and dried

Preheat oven to 275°F.

Heat the olive oil in a large nonstick frying pan, add 3 of the turkey chops and 3 of the garlic cloves, and brown them on all sides for about 2 minutes per side over medium heat. Transfer the chops to a roasting pan and repeat with remaining chops and garlic, adding more oil if needed. Combine the salt and pepper and rub the mixture into both sides of the turkey chop. Run the garlic through a garlic press and spread each chop with a portion of the mashed garlic. Cover the chops with buttered aluminum foil, and bake them for 15 minutes.

Pour the balsamic vinegar into the frying pan and boil to reduce to 1 tablespoon. Stir in the honey and mustard, and simmer for 5 minutes or until the liquid has the consistency of syrup. Add the Beef Stock and simmer for 10 minutes. Whisk the butter into the sauce a piece at a time.

Transfer the chops to a cutting board, strain the pan juices into the sauce, and cut the turkey chops into ½-inch strips.

Divide the salad greens among 6 dinner plates, place some turkey strips in the center of each plate, and spoon the sauce on top.

Turkey Chops with Tart Cherries

This is a great recipe for entertaining. The tart cherries gives the dish elegance without making it difficult.

Makes 6 servings

1 tablespoon sugar
¼ cup sherry vinegar
½ cup Port wine
1 package (4 ounces) pitted, dried tart cherries (available in specialty stores)
6 boneless turkey chops, each about 6 ounces and 1 inch thick
Salt and freshly ground pepper to taste
5 tablespoons butter, approximately
3 leeks, roots and all but 3 inches of dark green removed, cut in half lengthwise, rinsed thoroughly, and cut diagonally into 1-inch pieces
2 cups Beef Stock (page 152) or Chicken Stock (page 155)

Place the sugar and vinegar in a large skillet over moderate heat and cook until the mixture turns brown. Remove from the heat and, averting your face to protect against a flare-up, add the wine, bring to a boil, and stir until the candylike sugar has dissolved. Remove from the heat, add the cherries, and marinate for at least 2 hours. Strain and reserve marinade for the sauce.

Season the turkey chops on both sides with salt and black pepper. Melt 2 tablespoons of the butter in a large nonstick frying pan. When the butter starts to foam, brown the chops, 3 at a time, for 5 minutes per side. Transfer the chops to a cutting board, cover with aluminum foil, add more butter if needed, and repeat with the remaining chops.

In the same frying pan, melt 1 tablespoon of the butter, and stir-fry the leeks for 5 minutes. Remove and set aside. Add the marinade and the Beef Stock and simmer until reduced by half. Season to taste with additional salt and pepper, and add the cherries.

Carve the turkey chops into ½-inch strips. Place a mound of leeks in the center of each of 6 dinner plates, fan the turkey strips on top of the leeks, and spoon the sauce on top.

Turkey Tenderloin with Anchovy Pesto

After several fiascoes, I now pay close attention to the broiling process. The turkey is mostly cooked before it gets to the oven, where the broiler crisps the anchovy pesto.

Makes 6 servings

1 cup Italian (flat-leaf) parsley leaves, washed and dried
2 tablespoons pine nuts
2 cloves garlic
1 jar (4 ounces) roasted peppers, drained
12 anchovy fillets
1 tomato, about ½ pound, halved and seeded
¼ cup olive oil, plus a bit for preparing the pan
Pinch of dried oregano
1 tablespoon red wine vinegar
3 tablespoons plain bread crumbs
6 turkey tenderloins of even size, about 2¼ pounds
Salt and freshly ground black pepper to taste
4 tablespoons (½ stick) butter

Make a pesto by placing the parsley, pine nuts, and garlic in the workbowl of a food processor and pulsing for 10 seconds. Add the roasted peppers, anchovies, and tomato, and pulse again. With the machine running, add the ¼ cup of olive oil in a thin stream to make a paste. Transfer to a bowl, and stir in the oregano, vinegar, and bread crumbs.

Preheat oven to 400°F and lightly brush a broiler pan with a bit of additional olive oil.

Sprinkle the tenderloins with salt and pepper. Melt 2 tablespoons of the butter in a medium nonstick frying pan and brown 3 of the tenderloins for 2 minutes on each of the 3 surfaces. Place the browned tenderloins in the broiler pan. Wipe the frying pan with paper towels, melt the remaining 2 tablespoons of butter, and brown the remaining tenderloins. Transfer the tenderloins to the broiler pan, cover the pan with aluminum foil, and bake for 8 minutes. Remove promptly.

Set the oven rack on the second notch from top, and preheat the broiler.

Spread each tenderloin with a thick layer of anchovy pesto and broil, 6 inches from the heat for 1 minute. Leave the oven door ajar and pay close attention to the broiling to make sure that the pesto does not burn. Transfer the tenderloins to a cutting board, and slice into 1-inch-thick medallions. Arrange the medallions on preheated plates and drizzle with the pan drippings.

Turkey Tenderloin Rolls with Blueberries

The turkey tenderloins are so delicate that they must be cooked carefully. Browning the turkey slices in olive oil adds color and an interesting flavor.

Makes 6 servings

4 turkey tenderloins of even size, about
    2¼ pounds total
Salt and freshly ground black pepper to
    taste
¼ cup extra-virgin olive oil
2 tablespoons shallots, minced
¼ pound ground turkey meat
¼ pound chicken livers
2 tablespoons butter
1 tablespoon sugar
½ cup Port wine
2 cups Beef Stock (page 152)
1 tablespoon grated orange zest
1 cinnamon stick
Lemon juice to taste
1 cup blueberries, rinsed

Cut the turkey tenderloins horizontally into 3 slices of even thickness, sprinkle the slices lightly with salt and pepper, and coat both sides with 3 tablespoons of the olive oil. Cover with clear plastic wrap, and refrigerate for 1 hour.

Heat the remaining 1 tablespoon of olive oil in a large nonstick frying pan, and cook the shallots over low heat until soft. Add the ground turkey and chicken livers, sprinkle with additional salt and pepper,

increase the heat, and brown for about 10 minutes. Transfer to the workbowl of a food processor, and purée.

Preheat oven to 400°F.

While the oven is heating, spread the turkey slices evenly with the purée, roll them up lengthwise, and secure them with toothpicks.

Wipe the frying pan with a paper towel, place the pan over medium heat, and cook the turkey rolls in batches until they are brown all around, about 5 minutes. Transfer the rolls to a baking dish, cover with aluminum foil, and bake for 10 minutes.

In the same frying pan, melt the butter, add the sugar, and stir over low heat until the sugar caramelizes. Remove the pan from the heat, add the wine, Beef Stock, orange zest, and cinnamon stick. Simmer the sauce to reduce by half. Remove the cinnamon stick and season with additional salt and pepper and with the lemon juice. Add the blueberries, and turn off heat.

Remove the toothpicks from the rolls, cut each roll into 4 pieces, spoon some sauce on each of 6 preheated dinner plates, and arrange the turkey pieces, cut side up, in a circle on each plate.

Turkey Tenderloin with Cloves and Orange Sauce

The steps involved in preparing this dish are few and uncomplicated. Brown the turkey tenderloins and while they finish cooking in the oven, assemble the sauce using the same skillet.

Makes 6 servings

6 turkey tenderloins of even size, about 2¼ pounds
Salt and freshly ground black pepper to taste
4 tablespoons (½ stick) butter, approximately
1 can (6 ounces) frozen orange juice concentrate
2 cups Beef Stock (page 152)
1 tablespoon balsamic vinegar
3 tablespoons soy sauce
¼ teaspoon ground cloves
3 navel oranges, peeled and white pith removed, and each cut in 8 segments
Romaine lettuce leaves, rolled, then cut in fine shreds

Preheat oven to 400°F.

Lightly season the turkey tenderloins with salt and pepper. Heat 2 tablespoons of the butter in a large nonstick frying pan until foaming. Brown 3 of the tenderloins over high heat for about 2 minutes on each of the 3 surfaces, until brown all around. Transfer the browned tenderloins to a baking pan, and repeat with the remaining tenderloins, adding more butter to the frying pan if needed. Cover the baking pan with buttered aluminum foil, and bake for 12 minutes. Remove to a cutting board.

Add the orange juice concentrate, Beef Stock, and balsamic vinegar to the frying pan, bring to a boil, and, over high heat, reduce by half. Add the soy sauce and cloves, and simmer for 10 minutes. Season with additional salt and pepper, add the orange segments, and briefly reheat the sauce.

Cut the tenderloins into 1-inch medallions, arrange on each of 6 dinner plates, spoon some sauce on top, and garnish with the shredded lettuce.

Turkey Tenderloin
with Fresh Figs and Port Wine Sauce

This dish is sinfully rich and I prepare it only when well-ripened figs are available. But the flavors go together so well that it's worth the occasional extravagance.

Makes 6 servings

6 turkey tenderloins of even size, about
    2¼ pounds
Salt to taste
1 teaspoon freshly ground black pepper
¼ cup flour
6 to 8 tablespoons butter
1 shallot, minced
2 large carrots, cut into julienne
¼ cup dry white wine
2 cups Beef Stock (page 152)
6 fresh mission figs, cleaned carefully so
    as not to bruise skins
2 tablespoons sugar
½ cup Port wine

Cut each tenderloin horizontally into 3 slices of even thickness, sprinkle the pieces with salt and pepper, and dredge them in the flour. Heat 2 tablespoons of the butter in a large nonstick frying pan over medium heat, and brown the turkey slices, in batches, for about 30 seconds per side. Add a bit more butter for each new batch. Transfer the turkey slices to a plate and cover with aluminum foil.

Wipe the frying pan with paper towels, melt 1 tablespoon of butter, and add the minced shallot. Cook until shallot is soft, then add the julienned carrots. Cook until tender, but still firm, about 3 minutes. Transfer to the plate with the turkey and cover.

Pour the white wine into the same frying pan, and boil until volume is reduced to about 1 tablespoon. Add the Beef Stock and reduce by one-third of its original volume. Adjust salt. Slowly whisk in 2 tablespoons of butter, cut into small pieces. Remove pan from heat.

Place the figs stem side up on a cutting board. Cut into quarters, but do not cut through the bottom. Spread out the cut segments.

Melt the sugar and 1 tablespoon of butter in a medium saucepan over low heat until the sugar is caramelized. Remove the pan from heat, add the Port wine, return the pan to medium heat and stir until smooth. Add the figs and simmer gently until the sauce has the consistency of syrup. Transfer the figs to a plate and stir the syrup into the sauce.

Arrange the turkey slices on each of 6 warmed dinner plates, and sprinkle with the carrot julienne. Spoon the sauce on top and garnish each serving with a cut fig.

Turkey Tenderloin
with Ginger and Honey Sauce

Ginger is the main flavor source in this recipe. It's another dish whose simplicity and speed make it ideal for a dinner party.

Makes 6 servings

6 tablespoons butter
6 turkey tenderloins of even size, about
*   2¼ pounds*
Salt and freshly ground black pepper to
*   taste*
2 cups Beef Stock (page 152)
¼ cup honey
2 tablespoons honey mustard
¼ cup grated fresh gingerroot
1 teaspoon lemon juice
Minced fresh chives, for garnish

Preheat oven to 400°F.

Heat 2 tablespoons of the butter in a large nonstick frying pan, and brown 3 of the tenderloins over moderate heat for 1 minute on each of the three surfaces. Season lightly with salt and pepper, transfer them to a baking pan, and cover with buttered aluminum foil. Wipe the frying pan with paper towels, melt 2 tablespoons of the remaining butter, and brown the 3 remaining tenderloins. Transfer the browned tenderloins to the baking pan, cover with aluminum foil, and bake for 10 minutes. Remove from the oven and keep covered.

Add the Beef Stock, honey, honey mustard, and gingerroot to the frying pan, and boil to reduce liquid by half. Strain the sauce, return it to the pan, and whisk the remaining 2 tablespoons of butter, cut in small pieces, into the sauce, keeping the heat at its lowest setting. Season to taste with additional salt and freshly ground black pepper, and add the lemon juice.

Cut the turkey tenderloins on the bias into thin slices, and arrange the slices in the centers of each of 6 warmed dinner plates. Add the pan juices to the sauce, reheat, and spoon the sauce on top of the turkey. Sprinkle the minced chives on top.

Turkey Tenderloin with Lemon and Crisp Sage

Although sage is the traditional herb used for so many turkey recipes, you'll enjoy the most untraditional way it's used here.

Makes 6 servings

6 turkey tenderloins of even size, about
   2¼ pounds
2 tablespoons olive oil, plus additional for
   coating the pan
1 teaspoon ground sage
½ teaspoon grated lemon zest
1 teaspoon salt
1 teaspoon freshly ground black pepper
½ cup dry white wine
2 cups Beef Stock (page 152)
5 tablespoons butter
36 medium to large fresh sage leaves

Preheat oven to 400°F.

Coat the tenderloins on all surfaces with the olive oil. Combine the ground sage, lemon zest, salt, and pepper and rub into all surfaces of the meat. Cover with plastic wrap and refrigerate for 1 hour.

Heat a large cast-iron skillet, and brush with a bit of additional olive oil. Brown the tenderloins on each side until golden, about 1 minute on each of the 3 surfaces. Place the browned tenderloins in a baking pan and repeat with the remaining tenderloins. Cover with aluminum foil, and bake for 12 minutes.

Pour the wine into the skillet and boil until it is reduced to 1 tablespoon. Add the stock and reduce liquid by half its original volume. Season to taste with additional salt and pepper. Simmer and whisk in 3 tablespoons of the butter, cut into small pieces. Remove from heat.

Shake the sage leaves and tap them on the kitchen counter, but do not wash them. Melt 1 tablespoon of the remaining butter in a medium nonstick frying pan and add half the leaves. Sprinkle with a pinch of additional salt, and fry the leaves over medium to high heat until crisp, turning them once. Drain on paper towels. Wipe the frying pan, add the remaining butter, sage leaves, and another pinch of salt, and fry the second batch of leaves until crisp, turning them once. Transfer to paper towels.

Slice the tenderloins into thin slices and arrange them on each of 6 dinner plates. Reheat the sauce and spoon some over each serving. Place some crisp sage leaves on top and serve immediately.

Turkey Tenderloin with Sweet and Sour Quince

Quince is one of those ingredients that needs cooking to change its basic taste. Raw, they have an unpleasant tannic flavor, but cooking releases their delicate fragrance and gives them a nice blush.

Makes 6 servings

2 quince
½ cup cider vinegar
½ cup dry white wine
½ cup sugar
1 cinnamon stick
1 bay leaf
¼ inch fresh gingerroot
2 whole cloves
6 turkey tenderloins of even size, about
*   2 ¼ pounds*
1 teaspoon salt
Freshly ground black pepper to taste
¼ cup flour
3 tablespoons butter
3 tablespoons safflower oil
1 cup buttermilk
1 cup Beef Stock (page 152)
1 tablespoon cornstarch mixed with 2
*   tablespoons water*

Wash, peel, quarter, and remove the core from each quince. Cut each quarter into three wedges. Place the quince and the peelings with the core into a medium saucepan with 2 cups water. Bring to a boil and simmer for 15 minutes. Cover the pot, and let it sit overnight. When you resume

cooking, set the quince wedges aside, strain the liquid and reserve 2 cups, and discard the peels and core.

Combine the quince liquid, vinegar, white wine, sugar, cinnamon, bay leaf, ginger, and cloves, and simmer in the saucepan for 10 minutes. Add the quince wedges in a single layer, and simmer for 20 minutes more. Remove the quince with a slotted spoon, strain the liquid, and boil to reduce to 1 cup.

Preheat oven to 400°F.

Sprinkle the tenderloins on both sides with the salt and pepper. Roll the turkey tenderloins in the flour, and shake off any excess. Heat half the butter and oil in a Dutch oven on the stovetop, and brown the tenderloins in batches of 3 until they are golden brown all around. Transfer the browned tenderloins to a plate and continue browning the remaining tenderloins, wiping pan with paper towels before adding more butter and oil. Return all the tenderloins to the Dutch oven, and turn up the heat, on the stovetop, to medium. Add the buttermilk, quince liquid, and Beef Stock. Cover and place in the oven for 10 minutes.

Remove the tenderloins to a cutting board and cover with aluminum foil. Place the sauce over medium heat on the stovetop, and stir in cornstarch mixture. Simmer until lightly thickened. Season to taste with additional salt and black pepper. Carve the tenderloins on the bias into ½-inch slices, arrange them on each of 6 warmed dinner plates, garnish with the quince wedges, and spoon warm sauce on top.

Turkey Breast
with Gewürztraminer and Green Relish

Because of the high oven temperature, the cooking time for this turkey breast is short. However, you need a clean oven and a good exhaust fan to prevent too much smoke.

Makes 6 servings

2 tablespoons Clarified Butter (page 156)
1 whole turkey breast, about 5½ pounds
1 tablespoon salt
1 tablespoon freshly ground black pepper
2 cups Gewürztraminer wine
3 tablespoons minced chives
½ cup minced Italian (flat-leaf) parsley
1 large sour pickle, minced
3 anchovy filets, minced
2 tablespoons minced onion
1 clove garlic, minced
2 tablespoons capers, drained
¼ cup olive oil
1 tablespoon red wine vinegar
Freshly ground black pepper to taste
2 cups Chicken Stock (page 155) or
*   canned chicken broth*
2 leeks, roots and all but 2 inches of dark
*   greens removed, rinsed and cut into*
*   julienne pieces*
2 large carrots, cut into julienne
2 stalks celery, cut into julienne

Preheat oven to 475°F.

Place the Clarified Butter in a large Dutch oven or roasting pan. Rub the turkey breast inside and out with the salt and pepper, and brown it on the stovetop, breast side down, until golden. Turn breast side up and add 1 cup of the Gewürztraminer. Place in the oven, uncovered, and roast for 20 minutes, basting every 5 minutes or so with the pan juices. Add the remaining wine and cook 20 minutes more, again basting with pan juices every 5 minutes. If the skin browns too quickly, cover the breast loosely with aluminum foil.

Blend the chives, parsley, pickle, anchovies, onion, garlic, and capers briefly in the workbowl of a food processor. With the machine running, add the olive oil in a slow, steady stream, stir in the vinegar, and season with the black pepper.

Transfer the turkey breast to a carving board and cover with aluminum foil. Place the roasting pan over medium heat on the stovetop, and add the stock, leeks, carrots, and celery. Bring to a boil, reduce heat, and simmer for 8 minutes. Turn off the heat.

Skin the turkey breast and separate the breast from the bone in a single piece. Carve on the bias into ¼-inch-thick slices. Cover with aluminum foil.

Just before serving, reheat the vegetables and the sauce. Remove the vegetables with a slotted spoon and divide among 6 large soup plates. Place the turkey slices on top and ladle some cooking juices over the meat. Top with 1 tablespoon of the relish and serve the remaining at the table.

Soups

For most of my adult life, I stayed away from preparing soups. As with most food phobias, this one traced back to childhood. For me, soups were the vehicle for using up leftovers, and for me and most foods, the first time was enough, thank you. All those hated, overcooked vegetables would go into the soup pot, only to be cooked some more—and then puréed. Yikes!

But years later, I started making soups, and I took great care to select simple ingredients that were pleasing to the eye. Whenever the base needed to be puréed, I wouldn't purée more than one main ingredient. I merely poached the fish and seafood in the all-important homemade stock and added them in pieces just before serving.

Make a light lunch out of the nourishing vegetable chowder or start a meal on a hot summer day with a red pepper gazpacho.

All soups can be prepared ahead with quick last-minute assembling.

Artichoke Soup with Mint

I'm very fond of the flavor combination in this soup. The mint gives the gentle acidity of the artichoke an appealing flavor, and the canned artichokes are the sort of high-quality prepared products that I like to use. I've made the soup with fresh artichokes, which had a bit more flavor and a better texture, but the additional preparation work was substantial. You'll be very happy with this soup as it's presented here.

Makes 4 to 6 servings

2 cans (14 ounces each) artichoke
*   bottoms*
3 tablespoons butter
2 tablespoons flour
1 quart Vegetable Stock (page 164) or
*   canned chicken broth*
1 cup fresh mint leaves, rinsed
Pinch of cayenne pepper
Pinch of nutmeg
Salt to taste
Additional mint leaves, for garnish

Drain the artichokes, reserving 1 cup of the brine. Coarsely chop all but 3 of the artichoke bottoms, reserving the 3 for garnish.

Melt the butter in a large saucepan, stir in the flour, blend well, and simmer for 2 minutes. Slowly add the stock, whisking vigorously to prevent lumps from forming. Bring to the boil, and add the chopped artichokes. Add the 1 cup of mint leaves and simmer, covered, for 30 minutes.

Strain the soup into a large saucepan, and transfer the solids to the workbowl of a food processor. Purée in small batches. Return the puréed solids to the strained soup liquid, add the reserved artichoke brine, season with the cayenne and nutmeg, and blend well. Reheat and add salt.

Cut the reserved artichoke bottoms into ¼-inch wedges, and divide the wedges among 4 or 6 soup bowls. Ladle the soup over the wedges, and serve garnished with the additional mint leaves. This soup can also be served chilled.

Barley Soup with Oysters

The vegetables in this soup get only brief cooking. That keeps them crisp and creates an interesting texture contrast with the buttery oysters. When the oysters are opened, they release liquid that you'll use to enhance the flavor of the soup. Be sure to buy very fresh oysters and ask the fishmonger to shuck them for you. Just be sure to save the liquid.

Makes 6 servings

1 cup Fish Stock (page 158) or bottled
  clam juice
18 oysters, freshly shucked and liquid
  reserved
3 cups Chicken Stock (page 155) or
  canned chicken broth
1 medium carrot, cut into julienne
1 stalk celery, cut into julienne
1 or 2 small leeks, cut into ½-inch pieces,
  enough for 1 cup (see note)
2 tablespoons barley, rinsed
1 tablespoon lemon juice
Salt and freshly ground black pepper to
  taste
Cayenne pepper, for garnish

Bring the Fish Stock or clam juice to a boil in a large saucepan. Add the oysters and their liquid, and simmer for 1 minute. Remove the pan from the heat immediately, and cover, keeping the oysters in the liquid until you're ready to use them.

Bring the Chicken Stock to a boil, add the carrot and celery julienne, and simmer for 2 minutes. Remove the vegetables with a slotted spoon and place them in a bowl. Simmer the leek pieces in the stock for 1 minute, then remove them with the slotted spoon, and add them to the bowl with the carrots and celery.

Remove the oysters from the Fish Stock with a slotted spoon. Strain the Fish Stock into the Chicken Stock and bring to a boil. Add the barley and simmer for 35 minutes. Adjust the seasoning by adding the lemon juice, salt, and black pepper. Remove from the heat.

Divide the oysters and vegetables among 6 preheated soup bowls. Reheat the soup, and pour it into the soup bowls, give each serving a light dusting of cayenne pepper, and serve.

Note: To prepare the leeks, cut off the roots, remove the tough outer leaves, and trim the tops, leaving 5 inches of the green part. Cut in half lengthwise and rinse under cold running water, spreading the leaves to rinse off soil lodged in between. Then cut on the bias into ½-inch pieces.

Celery Root Soup with Caviar Toast

This soup is best when it's prepared a day in advance. Refrigerate the soup after you've puréed it and prepare the *crème fraîche,* which also needs to sit overnight. While you reheat the soup for serving, you can prepare the caviar toasts.

Makes 6 servings

2 tablespoons butter
2 tablespoons minced shallots
2 pounds celery root, dark skin removed
*   and cut in medium dice*
1½ quarts Vegetable Stock (page 164) or
*   canned chicken broth*
Salt to taste
12 slices French bread (baguette) each
*   ½ inch thick*
1 ounce salmon roe (any variety,
*   including the inexpensive ones)*
6 tablespoons minced chives
6 tablespoons crème fraîche (page 157) or
*   sour cream*
Cayenne pepper to taste

Preheat oven to 350°F.

Melt the butter in a large saucepan and cook the shallots over low heat until they are softened, about 5 minutes. Add the diced celery root and stir. Add the stock, bring to the boil, then reduce heat and simmer, covered, for 1 hour. Strain the soup into another saucepan, and transfer the solids to the workbowl of a food processor. Purée in small batches and return to soup. Add salt.

Place the bread slices on a cookie sheet and bake in the oven for 5 minutes. Let cool on a rack. Combine the salmon roe, chives, and *crème fraîche,* and spread the mixture on the toasted bread slices.

Reheat the soup and divide among 6 soup bowls, each lightly dusted with cayenne. Pass the toasts at the table.

Cucumber-Rice Soup with Mint

Cucumber and mint are great summer ingredients, as this delicious soup demonstrates. The lime juice adds its own summery spark, and the soup can be served hot or cold. The rice makes the soup heartier.

Makes 6 servings

¼ cup basmati rice
3 cucumbers, peeled, seeded, halved
    lengthwise, and cut in ½-inch slices
1 tablespoon butter
1 medium onion, coarsely chopped
6 cups Vegetable Stock (page 164) or
    canned chicken broth
1 cup mint leaves, stems removed, rinsed,
    and chopped
3 tablespoons fresh lime juice
Salt and freshly ground black pepper to
    taste
Mint sprigs, rinsed, for garnish

Rinse the rice, cover with cold water, and set aside for 30 minutes. Sprinkle 1 cup of the cucumber pieces with a pinch of salt, and set aside to be added at the end.

Melt the butter in a Dutch oven on the stovetop and cook the onion, without browning, over the lowest possible heat for 30 minutes. Add the stock and bring to a boil. Drain the rice and add to the liquid with the remaining 2 cups of cucumber and the chopped mint. Bring to a boil, reduce to a simmer, and cook for 30 minutes.

Strain the soup. Reserve the liquid, and purée the solids in several batches in a food processor. Return the purée to the soup, reheat, stir in the lime juice and season with salt and pepper.

Squeeze any excess water from the reserved cucumbers, and divide them among 6 soup bowls. Pour soup into each bowl and garnish with the mint sprigs. Serve hot or cold.

Curried Mussel Soup with Leek

If you like the sound of this recipe, let it serve double duty. As an alternative to soup, omit the fish stock and serve the mussels, in their shell, over 1 pound of your favorite cooked pasta.

Makes 6 servings

2 pounds fresh, cultivated mussels, scrubbed and debearded
1 large tomato, cut in half horizontally, seeds and excess juice removed, cut in small dice
1 teaspoon olive oil
1 clove garlic, mashed
Salt and freshly ground black pepper to taste
2 tablespoons butter
2 tablespoons minced onions
½ cup dry, white vermouth
1 quart Fish Stock (page 158) or bottled clam juice
2 tablespoons cider vinegar
½ teaspoon curry powder
1 large leek, cleaned and cut in strips (see note)

Discard any mussels that are broken or already open. Toss the diced tomatoes with the olive oil and mashed garlic, season with salt and pepper, cover and set aside.

Melt the butter in a large saucepan, cook the onions until they are translucent, add the vermouth, and bring to the boil. Add the mussels, then cover the pan and cook, shaking the pan occasionally until all the mussels have opened, about 8 to 10 minutes. Remove the mussels with a slotted spoon and, when they are cool enough to handle, remove the shells. Discard any mussels that did not open. Strain the cooking liquid through a sieve lined with cheesecloth. Rinse the pan and return the strained liquid to it.

Add the stock, vinegar, and curry to the liquid, and cook over moderate heat for 10 minutes. Add the leek strips and cook for 2 minutes. Taste, and adjust the seasoning with salt and pepper.

Divide the mussels among 6 soup bowls. Ladle the hot soup over mussels and garnish with the diced tomato mixture.

Note: To prepare the leeks, cut off the roots, remove the tough outer leaves, and trim the tops, leaving 5 inches of the green part. Cut in half lengthwise and rinse under cold running water, spreading the leaves to rinse off soil lodged in between. Then cut on the bias into ½-inch pieces.

Escarole Soup with Smoked Salmon

Powdered saffron loses its flavor quickly and is often cut with turmeric. A better ingredient is saffron in thread form. Yes, saffron threads are extremely expensive, but a couple of threads go a long way toward enhancing the flavor and color of a dish.

Makes 6 servings

¾ pound escarole, about 8 cups finely shredded
Zest of 1 lemon
2 tablespoons olive oil
¼ cup minced shallots
Pinch of salt
1 quart Chicken Stock (page 155) or canned chicken broth
¼ teaspoon saffron threads softened in 1 tablespoon cold water
Freshly ground black pepper to taste
12 slices low-salt smoked salmon, about ⅓ pound, cut in ¼-inch strips

Cut off and discard a small piece from the base of the escarole, then break off all the leaves, discarding any that are wilted or discolored. Rinse under cold running water and shred finely.

Bring about 1 quart of water to a boil in a small saucepan, cook the lemon zest for about 1 minute, and drain.

Heat the olive oil in a large saucepan, add the shallots, and cook until the shallots are lightly browned, about 5 minutes. Add the escarole and salt, sauté over high heat until the escarole is wilted, and transfer the escarole and shallots to a bowl. Add the stock, the saffron, and the saffron soaking water to the saucepan, simmer for 10 minutes, and season with freshly ground black pepper. (Depending on the saltiness of the salmon, additional salt may not be necessary.)

Divide the escarole, salmon strips, and lemon zest among 6 preheated soup bowls, and ladle the hot soup on top.

Fennel Soup with Shrimp

Shrimp shells contain a lot of flavor. A lot of people throw them away without thinking about that. Cooking the shrimp with their shell on is integral to this recipe, as is the use of the shells after the shrimp are peeled. They give the soup a stronger shrimp flavor.

Makes 6 servings

2 large fennel bulbs
¼ cup olive oil
12 extra-large shrimp
1 onion, chopped
1 large carrot, chopped
1 large stalk celery, chopped
1 teaspoon dried thyme
½ cup parsley leaves, chopped
2 tablespoons Pernod or other licorice-
*   flavored liqueur*
2 quarts Fish Stock (page 158) or bottled
*   clam juice*
Salt and freshly ground black pepper to
*   taste*
Minced fennel fronds, for garnish

Preheat oven to 425°F. Remove and discard the finger-like parts of the fennel bulbs. Reserve the fronds to use as a garnish. Remove the stringy outer layer of each fennel bulb with a vegetable peeler, cut each bulb in half, and cut each half into ¼-inch-thick slices.

Heat the olive oil in a Dutch oven on the stovetop. When the oil is almost smoking, add the shrimp, still in their shells, stir to coat, and brown on each side for 30 seconds. Stir in the onions, carrots, celery, thyme, and parsley. Roast in the oven, uncovered, for 10 minutes. Remove shrimp to a plate, and, when they're cool enough to handle, peel and devein them.

Place the shrimp shells, Pernod, and stock in the Dutch oven, and simmer on the stovetop for 30 minutes, or until the liquid has been reduced to 6 cups. Strain, season with salt and pepper, add the fennel slices, and cook for 1 minute.

Meanwhile, cut each shrimp in half horizontally and place the pieces in 6 soup bowls. Ladle the hot liquid on top and garnish with the minced fennel fronds.

Red Pepper Gazpacho with Hummus Toast

Countless soups can be called gazpacho because they use uncooked vegetables. In this one, the peppers aren't cooked so much as they are given a smoked flavor that pairs well with the other ingredients. Although it can be served hot, it's best, like most gazpachos, when chilled.

Makes 6 servings

6 roasted red bell peppers (page 161), about 2½ pounds total
2 cucumbers, seeds removed, and cut in small pieces
3 medium cloves garlic, put through a garlic press
2 cups Chicken Stock (page 155) or canned chicken broth
2 tablespoons olive oil
2 tablespoons lime-juice concentrate
Salt to taste
¼ teaspoon Tabasco sauce
1 bunch scallions, finely minced
12 slices French bread (baguette) each ½ inch thick
4 ounces hummus spread (storebought)
Grated Monterey Jack cheese

After you've peeled off the skins from the roasted peppers, cut the peppers in half, remove the seeds, and purée them and the cucumbers in 2 batches in the workbowl of a food processor.

Heat the stock, stir in the puréed vegetables and the mashed garlic, and mix in the olive oil, lime-juice concentrate, salt, Tabasco, and scallions. Refrigerate for 4 hours.

Just before serving, preheat the oven to 350°F, spread the bread slices with the hummus, and top with the grated cheese. Place on a cookie sheet, and bake for 10 minutes. Ladle the chilled soup into 6 bowls, and pass the toasts at the table with the soup.

Roasted Mushroom Soup with Scallion Toast

As you can see from the recipes in this chapter, I like accompanying my soups with compatible toasts. This is a good example. Although I usually make mayonnaise from scratch, for these scallion toasts I used a commercial brand.

Makes 6 servings

2 tablespoons flour
1½ quarts Chicken Stock (page 155) or
Mushroom Stock (page 159)
1 pound white mushrooms, cleaned and
sliced
1 cup dried porcini mushrooms, soaked
for 4 hours or overnight in 2 cups
water
1 cup fresh parsley, minced
Salt and freshly ground black pepper to
taste

Scallion toasts:
1 tablespoon Dijon mustard
Pinch of sugar
1 teaspoon lemon juice
3 scallions, minced
½ cup mayonnaise (storebought is
acceptable)
Salt and freshly ground black pepper to
taste
12 slices French bread (baguette) each
½ inch thick

Brown the flour in a large saucepan over moderate heat, stirring constantly, for about 10 minutes. Heat the stock in a separate saucepan. As soon as flour turns brown, remove it from the heat, let it cool for 1 minute, and add to it 1 cup of the hot stock, whisking constantly. Add the remaining stock and white mushrooms, and bring soup to a boil.

Drain the soaked porcini mushrooms and reserve the soaking liquid. Rinse each mushroom under cold running water, folding back the curled edges to remove any sand. Add to the soup. Strain the soaking liquid through a fine sieve or cheesecloth, and simmer, covered, until reduced to 1 quart. Strain the soup into a bowl, and discard the mushrooms. Stir in the minced parsley and season with salt and pepper.

To make the toasts, preheat oven to 375°F. Combine the mustard, sugar, lemon juice, and scallions, add to the mayonnaise, and season with salt and pepper. Spread 1 teaspoon of the flavored mayonnaise on each bread slice.

Place the slices on a cookie sheet, and brown in the oven for 8 minutes. Divide the soup among 6 bowls and serve accompanied by the scallion toasts.

Snow Pea Soup with Cod

Coriander is the seed of the cilantro plant. It has a light lemon flavor that works deliciously in a fish soup. This soup is exotic, easy to prepare, and low in fat.

Makes 6 servings

5 cloves garlic
1 tablespoon olive oil
½ pound fresh snow peas
3 cups bottled clam juice
4 cups water
2 tablespoons light yellow miso paste
1 ½ pounds cod steaks
¼ teaspoon freshly ground coriander
3 minced scallions
Salt and freshly ground black pepper to taste
Cheese-flavored Palmiers (page 160)

Preheat oven to 350°F. Dip the garlic cloves in the olive oil and roast the cloves on a baking sheet for 20 minutes. Remove the garlic, and reduce the oven temperature to the lowest setting.

Bring about 1 quart of salted water to a boil, add the snow peas, turn off heat, and let stand for 3 minutes. Drain and place the snow peas in ice water to set their color. Drain the peas.

In a large saucepan, make the soup by bringing the clam juice, the 4 cups of water, the miso paste, and the roasted garlic cloves to a boil. Reduce the heat, simmer for 5 minutes, and stir well to blend in the miso paste. Add the cod and simmer for 7 minutes. Transfer the fish to a plate and, when cool enough to handle, remove the skin and any bones. Break the fish into bite-size pieces, place on a plate, cover with aluminum foil, and keep warm in the oven.

Strain the fish soup, return to the saucepan, add the ground coriander and the minced scallions, and reheat. Adjust seasoning with salt and pepper.

Divide the snow peas and fish pieces among 6 preheated soup bowls, ladle some hot soup into each bowl, and serve accompanied with the cheese-flavored Palmiers.

Sweet Pea Soup with Monkfish

The puréed peas give this soup a striking color that contrasts beautifully with the fish. To highlight that contrast, I serve the soup in shallow soup plates, and ladle the soup in before adding the fish pieces.

Makes 6 servings

1½ quarts Fish Stock (page 158) or
bottled clam juice
1½ pounds boneless monkfish
2 tablespoons butter
1 large onion, peeled and cut into rings
2 packages (10 ounces each) frozen tiny
peas
1 tablespoon Pernod or other licorice-
flavored liqueur
2 tablespoons lemon juice
Salt and freshly ground black pepper to
taste
Fresh tarragon fronds, minced

Bring the Fish Stock or clam juice to a boil in a 3-quart saucepan. Add the monkfish, simmer for 15 minutes, remove the fish, and, when cool enough to handle, run your fingers over fish to detect and remove any bones. Set the fish aside, covered. Strain the stock into a clean saucepan, and add enough water to measure 1½ quarts.

Melt the butter in a Dutch oven on the stovetop, add the onion rings, cover, and sweat the onions over the lowest possible heat for about 20 minutes; do not brown the onions. Turn up the heat and add the stock. When the stock begins to boil, add the frozen peas and boil vigorously for 5 minutes. Strain and reserve liquid.

Transfer the solids to the workbowl of a food processor, purée in several batches, and strain through a coarse sieve, pushing the solids down with a spatula to use as much of the peas as possible. Discard any pea skins that remain in the sieve.

Bring the soup to a boil, and stir in the Pernod, lemon juice, salt, and pepper. Cut the fish into bite-size pieces, and divide among 6 preheated soup bowls. Ladle the boiling soup on top, and garnish with the tarragon fronds.

Vegetable Chowder en Croûte

This soup is so loaded with vegetables that it's a meal in itself. It's covered with a round of puff pastry that has been baked just before serving. The pastry gives the dish a spectacular look on the dinner table.

Makes 6 servings

2 tablespoons butter
1 medium onion, peeled and cut into
*   thin rings*
2 cups broccoli florets, broken into bite-
*   size pieces*
½ pound small red potatoes, scrubbed
*   and cut into eighths*
2 carrots, peeled and sliced ¼ inch thick
½ cup fresh basil leaves, minced, or 1
*   tablespoon dried basil*
1½ quarts Chicken Stock (page 155) or
*   canned chicken broth*
½ pound mushrooms with stems, cleaned
*   and thinly sliced*
Salt and freshly ground pepper to taste
2 sheets frozen puff pastry (9 x 9½
*   inches each)*
1 egg mixed with 1 tablespoon water

Melt the butter in a large Dutch oven on the stovetop, and cook the onion rings, covered, over the lowest possible heat for 30 minutes. Meanwhile, bring about 3 quarts of salted water to a boil in a large pot. Add the broccoli florets, cook for 3 minutes, drain, and rinse with cold water.

When the onions have cooked, raise the heat to medium and add the potatoes and carrots. If the basil you're using is dried, add it here. Cook, stirring frequently, for about 6 minutes. Add the stock and mushrooms, and simmer for 15 more minutes. Season with salt and pepper, divide the broccoli among 6 ovenproof soup cups, and ladle the soup on top. If you're using fresh basil, add it here. Refrigerate.

Allow the puff pastry to defrost for about 30 minutes, and gently unfold it. Roll out the sheets on a lightly floured surface, and cut out 6 round pieces large enough to overlap the soup cups by half an inch. Make an egg wash by whisking the egg and the water, and brush the outside rim of each soup cup with the egg wash. Drape the pastry rounds over the soup cups but don't let them touch the soup. Firmly press the pastry to the contour of the cups. (You can prepare this dish ahead to this point and refrigerate the cups.)

Preheat oven to 450°F.

Just before serving, brush the tops of the pastry with more of the egg wash, and gently draw a fork across the pastry tops to make a design. Place the soup cups on a baking sheet, and bake for 15 minutes or until the crust is golden. Serve immediately.

Yellow Tomato Soup with Anchovy Toast

This dish is a perfect example of how simple ingredients can create something special.

Makes 6 servings

1 tablespoon olive oil
2 shallots, chopped
1 clove garlic, put through a garlic press
3 pounds yellow tomatoes, skinned, cut in half horizontally, seeded, and puréed
1 quart Vegetable Stock (page 164) or canned chicken broth
Pinch of sugar
Pinch of nutmeg
1 tablespoon dry sherry
Salt and freshly ground black pepper to taste
Fresh basil leaves, cleaned, dried, and shredded

Anchovy Toasts:
¼ cup olive oil
1 tablespoon anchovy paste
1 tablespoon tomato paste
1 clove garlic, put through a garlic press
Freshly ground black pepper
12 slices French bread (baguette), each ½ inch thick

Place a large saucepan over low heat, add the olive oil, shallots, and garlic, and cook, stirring occasionally, over the lowest possible heat for 5 minutes. Add the puréed tomatoes, stock, sugar, nutmeg, and sherry. Mix the ingredients, and simmer, covered, for 30 minutes. Season with salt and pepper.

While the soup is simmering, preheat the oven to 350°F and make the anchovy toasts.

Whisk together the olive oil, anchovy paste, tomato paste, garlic, and black pepper. Brush a generous amount of the mixture on each of the bread slices, place the slices on a cookie sheet, and bake for 10 minutes. Remove the anchovy toasts from the oven and let cool on a rack.

When the soup has finished simmering, place 2 anchovy toasts into each soup bowl, ladle the hot soup over the toasts, and serve immediately, garnished with some shredded basil leaves.

Appetizers

Appetizers are meant to excite the palate and to set the mood for the main course. That's what I have tried to do with the dishes in this chapter. Most of them are made with a colorful salad base to which I have added a little fish or seafood.

Not all of them, though. I also have a vegetable terrine in these pages as well as a few light pastas.

But "light" is always the key word, so appetizers can build up to the main dish that follows. However, there's nothing to stop you from taking the theme a step further and serving a couple of these dishes as the full meal. Or let one of them become a light lunch. Or expand one of them by adding a soup and a dessert and calling it a meal.

Avocado with Shrimp

Your avocados need to be perfectly ripe. The best bet is to buy them three days before you'll use them. Ripening can be accelerated, if need be, by storing the avocados in a paper bag. Drizzle the cut avocado with lemon juice, but only right before serving, to prevent darkening of the buttery green flesh.

Makes 6 servings

18 large shrimp, peeled and deveined
2 tablespoons soy sauce
1 tablespoon lemon juice
2 tablespoons walnut oil
Zest of 1 orange, cut in julienne
½ cup safflower oil
¼ cup lemon juice
¼ teaspoon salt
Coarsely ground black pepper
2 tablespoons butter
2 medium avocados, perfectly ripe
2 heads Bibb or 1 head Boston lettuce,
*   rinsed and dried*
3 tablespoons shelled pistachios, coarsely
*   chopped*

Rinse the shrimp peels, place in a small saucepan, cover with cold water, and boil to reduce liquid to 2 tablespoons. Strain into a mixing bowl, add the soy sauce, lemon juice, and walnut oil, and blend. Add the shrimp and marinate in the refrigerator for 1 hour.

Meanwhile, bring about 1 cup of water to the boil in a small saucepan, add the strips of orange zest, and boil for 1 minute. Drain, and set aside on paper towels.

Make a dressing by blending the safflower oil, lemon juice, salt, and pepper.

Remove the shrimp from marinade and dry them with paper towels. Melt the butter in a large frying pan. When the butter begins to foam, add the shrimp and cook for 1 minute per side. Remove the shrimp. Pour the marinade into the frying pan, and boil until reduced to about 6 tablespoons.

Peel the avocados, cut each in half lengthwise, discard the pits, and slice diagonally into ⅛-inch-thick "half-moons." Divide the lettuce leaves among each of 6 plates, place some avocado slices in a circle on top, spoon the salad dressing on top, place 3 shrimp in the middle of each plate, and spoon the warm marinade on top. Sprinkle some pistachio bits and orange zest on top.

Baby Artichokes
with Carrots and Champagne Vinegar

With some recipes, there's just no substitute for fresh produce, and this is one of them—in this case, California baby artichokes. They have a very short growing season, so when early summer comes around, plan for their subtle, nutty flavor.

Makes 6 servings

4 cloves garlic
¼ cup olive oil
2 pounds California baby artichokes,
    24 to 30 pieces
2 cups carrots, peeled and cut into
    julienne strips
½ cup champagne vinegar
¼ cup Chicken Stock (page 155) or
    canned chicken broth
1 teaspoon salt
1 teaspoon freshly ground black pepper

Preheat oven to 350°F.

Dip the garlic cloves in the olive oil, place on a cookie sheet, bake for 15 minutes, peel, and mash with a fork.

Cut the stems at base of the artichoke bulbs and slice off ½ inch from the tops. Remove three to four layers of outer leaves to expose the smooth, yellow part of each artichoke.

Heat the olive oil in a Dutch oven, add the mashed garlic and julienned carrots, and sauté over high heat for 3 minutes, stirring constantly. Place the artichokes upright on top of the carrots, and pour the champagne vinegar and stock on top. Bring to a boil, reduce heat, add salt and pepper, cover the pan, and simmer for 25 minutes. Turn off heat and let stand, covered, until cooled.

Remove the artichokes from the pan, and slice them in half vertically. Place them cut sides up on a serving plate and top each half with some julienned carrot. Spoon some pan juices on top, and serve at room temperature or chilled.

Cucumber Wheels
with Crabmeat and Sushi Rice

The pickled ginger and wasabi give this dish an unmistakable Japanese flavor, but beyond that, I've taken a lot of liberties in preparing my version of Japanese sushi rolls.

Makes 6 servings

4 cucumbers
¼ teaspoon salt
½ pound lump or backfin crabmeat
2 tablespoons soy sauce
2 tablespoons fresh lime juice
1 teaspoon lime zest, grated
1 tablespoon honey
⅓ cup sushi rice (Japanese short-grain rice)
1 cup plus 2 tablespoons water
1 tablespoon sushi rice vinegar (flavored rice vinegar)
3 tablespoons minced pickled ginger
2 tablespoons wasabi powder mixed with 1½ tablespoons water
6 tablespoons soy sauce

Peel the cucumbers, and cut off ½ inch from each end. Cut in half across the middle. With the tip of a vegetable peeler, root out the seeds, working toward the middle from each end. Rub the cucumbers inside and out with the salt, and stand them on end on a plate to drain for 30 minutes or longer.

Pick through the crabmeat to remove any pieces of shell. Squeeze out any excess liquid and place the crabmeat in a bowl.

Whisk together the soy sauce, lime juice, lime zest, and honey, pour the mixture over the crabmeat, mix, and refrigerate for 3 hours.

Soak the rice in a bowl of cold water, mix, and, when the water becomes cloudy, drain and soak again. Repeat until the water runs clear. Let drain for at least 30 minutes.

Place the rice in a Dutch oven and add the water. Cover the pan and set over medium heat. Bring the rice water to a boil, and cook, without lifting the lid, for 2 minutes. Reduce the heat and cook 5 minutes more, then turn off the heat and let the rice stand, covered, to steam for 15 minutes. Remove the lid and let the rice cool. Place the rice in a bowl with the rice vinegar and pickled ginger. Blend well.

Mix the wasabi powder and the water, and set aside for 5 minutes. Shape into a ball.

Dry the cucumbers with paper towels. Squeeze out any excess marinade from the crabmeat and reserve. Working towards the middle of the hollowed-out cucumbers, fill 4 cucumber halves with the crab mixture, packing it tightly. Fill the remaining cucumber halves with rice and slice into ½-inch rounds. Divide among 6 plates and drizzle with the marinade. Whisk the wasabi with the soy sauce until smooth, and serve for dipping.

65

Fennel with Smoked Salmon

So many of the best dishes are so good because they take advantage of contrasts. This wonderful hors d'oeuvre is one, with the crisp fennel playing off the buttery smoked salmon. I also like lots of the bold rich flavor of tellicherry peppercorns, ground extra coarse, on the salmon.

Makes 6 servings

¼ cup olive oil
1 tablespoon lime juice
¼ teaspoon salt
Freshly ground tellicherry pepper to taste
2 bulbs fennel, about 2 pounds
12 large but thin-cut slices of smoked
    salmon
2 tablespoons tiny capers
1 tablespoon balsamic vinegar
Pumpernickel bread

Combine the olive oil and lime juice, and season with salt and pepper.

Set aside the best fennel ferns for garnish. Use only the bulb of the fennel for the recipe; reserve the stalks for another use. Using a vegetable peeler, remove the stringy outer layer of the bulb. Cut off and discard a ½-inch-thick slice from the base of the bulb. Starting at the base, cut the fennel into paper-thin slices using either a mandoline or the thin (1 mm) slicing disc of a food processor. Toss immediately with the oil-lime juice to prevent the fennel from discoloring. Set aside at room temperature for 1 hour.

Just before serving, line 6 dinner plates with a thin layer of fennel slices. Sprinkle one side of the salmon slices with ground tellicherry pepper, roll up the slices, and place 2 slices in the center of each plate. Sprinkle some capers on top, drizzle with the balsamic vinegar, and garnish with the reserved fennel ferns. Serve accompanied by the pumpernickel.

Fettuccine with Smoked Salmon and Escarole Sauce

This colorful pasta dish served with crusty bread makes a perfect lunch. If fresh fettuccine is not available, the thinnest spaghetti made from durum wheat is an acceptable substitute.

Makes 6 servings

2 pounds fresh escarole
Zest of 1 lemon, cut in julienne
2 tablespoons butter
Salt and freshly ground black pepper to
*   taste*
12 ounces fresh egg fettuccine, made
*   from durum wheat*
½ cup Chicken Stock (page 155) or
*   Vegetable Stock (page 164)*
8 ounces low-salt smoked salmon slices,
*   cut into 1-inch strips*

Remove any tough or wilted outer leaves from the escarole, cut off and discard a thin slice from the bottom, and remove the leaves individually. Rinse well and place in tepid water for 10 minutes. Bring about 6 quarts of salted water to a boil, add the escarole, and boil for 2 minutes. Drain the escarole, refresh it with cold water, squeeze out excess moisture, and chop it coarsely.

Bring about 1 quart of water to a boil, cook the lemon zest for 1 minute, drain, and rinse it with cold water. Set aside on paper towels.

Melt the butter in a large saucepan and cook the escarole over moderate heat for 2 minutes. Sprinkle with salt, pepper, and the lemon zest. Set aside.

Warm 6 dinner plates in oven at lowest setting.

Bring at least 6 quarts of salted water to a boil and cook the fettuccine for 2 minutes (or according to package directions if you're using dried pasta) or until al dente. Drain and rinse briefly with hot water. Return the pasta to the pot, blend with the escarole, and set over low heat. Heat the stock, pour over the fettuccine, add the salmon, and blend well. Place on warmed dinner plates and serve immediately.

Goat Cheese Napoleons

A napoleon is most often thought of as a dessert. But the same principles can turn a napoleon into a savory dish like this, with alternating layers of puff pastry, goat cheese, and tomatoes.

Makes 6 servings

1 sheet frozen puff pastry, 9 x 9½ inches
6 tablespoons grated Gruyère cheese
2 tablespoons butter
2 large tomatoes, about 2 pounds, peeled, seeded, and chopped
Salt and freshly ground black pepper to taste
1 sun-dried tomato in olive oil, minced, plus 1 teaspoon oil from the tomatoes
6 ounces goat cheese, such as Montrachet, crumbled
2 tablespoons chives, minced
Arugula leaves or baby greens, rinsed and dried

Preheat oven to 375°F.

Defrost the pastry sheet for 30 minutes. Gently unfold and cut along the perforated lines. Cut each strip in half across the middle to make 6 pieces, and place the pieces on an ungreased, nonstick cookie sheet. Prick the dough with a fork at 1-inch intervals, sprinkle the cheese over the top, and bake for 15 to 20 minutes, until the top is golden. Let cool on a rack.

Using a serrated knife, cut the pastries in half horizontally. Taking care not to damage the delicate pastry, remove the uncooked dough from the center, leaving only the crisp outer shell. You now have one plain (bottom part) and one with cheese (top part).

Melt the butter in a frying pan and sauté the tomato for 30 seconds. Sprinkle with salt and pepper, remove from the heat, and stir in the minced sun-dried tomato, the oil from the sun-dried tomato, the crumbled goat cheese, and the minced chives. Blend well.

Just before serving, place the bottom layers of the puff pastry on a plate and spread them with the goat cheese-tomato mixture. Cover with the pastry top and surround with the greens.

Salmon Fillets with Salmon Roe

Almost all chefs prefer sea salt or kosher salt to ordinary table salt. I find the difference most noticeable in seafood cooking. So whenever I cook fish, I use a good-quality sea salt. It dissolves more quickly and enhances the flavor naturally.

Makes 6 servings

6 fresh salmon fillets, about ¼ inch thick
    and 4 ounces each, skin removed
1 teaspoon sea salt
2 tablespoons melted butter
3 tablespoons butter
1 large shallot, minced
1 cup bottled clam juice
1 cup dry sparkling white wine
2 ounces salmon roe
2 tablespoons minced chives
Salt and freshly ground black pepper to
    taste
6 mini-bagels, halved and toasted

Brush a large glass baking dish with butter, place the salmon fillets into the dish in a single layer, sprinkle with the salt, and drizzle each fillet with some of the melted butter.

Melt 1 tablespoon of the whole butter and cook the shallots until they are translucent. Add the clam juice and sparkling wine, and cook over high heat to reduce the liquid to half its volume. Gradually stir in the remaining 2 tablespoons of butter, and cook over low heat until the sauce has thickened slightly.

Preheat the broiler and broil the salmon fillets 4 inches from the heat for 2 minutes. Remove promptly.

Just before serving, heat the sauce, stir in the salmon roe, minced chives, any juices from the baking dish, salt, and pepper. Arrange the salmon fillets on individual plates and top with sauce. Serve with the toasted bagel halves.

Salmon Fillets Wrapped in Seaweed

Even though it looks elegant, this is not a difficult dish. You'll find pre-toasted, dried seaweed and brown rice vinegar in Asian grocery stores or some supermarkets, and the sauce is a variation of a traditional beurre blanc.

Makes 6 servings

1½ pounds salmon fillet, skin removed, cut into 12 1¼ x 7 inch strips
½ teaspoon sea salt
3 leaves dried seaweed, each 7½ inches square
2 tablespoons brown rice vinegar
¼ cup dry white wine

Sauce:
½ cup dry white wine
½ cup dry white vermouth
2 large shallots, minced
2 sprigs parsley
1 cup bottled clam juice
1 teaspoon saffron threads, soaked in 1 tablespoon water
4 tablespoons (½ stick) butter, cut in pieces
Salt and freshly ground black pepper to taste
1 bunch watercress, rinsed and dried

Preheat oven to 350°F. Butter a large glass baking dish and one side of a large piece of wax paper.

Sprinkle the salmon with sea salt and cut into 12 portions. Place seaweed leaves on a dry surface and cut along marked lines to make 12 strips, each 1¼-inch-wide. Brush both sides of the strips with the brown rice vinegar. Place each salmon piece on a seaweed strip and form into a roll. Arrange the rolls, seaweed side up (to prevent the salmon from drying) in a single layer in a baking dish, pour the ¼ cup of wine over, cover with the wax paper, butter side down, and bake for 15 minutes.

To make the sauce, heat the ½ cup of wine and the ½ cup of vermouth in a saucepan with the shallots and the parsley sprigs, and reduce the liquid to about ¼ cup. Add the clam juice, any juices from the baking pan, and the saffron threads with their soaking liquid. Bring to a boil, and reduce the liquid to half its original volume. Strain, return the sauce to the pan over the lowest possible setting, and whisk in the butter a piece at a time. Season with the salt and pepper.

Divide the watercress among 6 preheated dinner plates, and center 2 pieces of salmon wrap on each plate. Spoon the sauce on top and serve immediately.

71

Sea Scallops and Green Beans with Watercress Sauce

Scallops cry out for a colorful complement on the plate. The green beans and watercress contribute perfect color and flavor to this dish. Select green beans that are small and that snap apart easily.

Makes 6 servings

1 pound very thin green beans
3 cups tightly packed watercress (1 to 2
*   bunches), rinsed, 6 sprigs reserved*
*   for garnish*
1 tablespoon butter
1 medium shallot, minced
¼ cup olive oil
2 tablespoons lime juice
Sea salt to taste
Pinch of cayenne pepper
12 sea scallops of even size, about 1
*   pound, small side muscles removed*

Bring about 3 quarts of salted water to a boil in a large saucepan. Stem the beans and cook them for 2 minutes. Drain the beans and plunge them into very cold water to stop the cooking and set their color. Bring about 1 quart of salted water to a boil and cook the watercress leaves for 2 minutes, drain, and rinse with cold water.

Melt the butter in a medium saucepan and cook the minced shallot over low heat until softened. Stir in the watercress leaves and cook until well blended. Purée in a food processor and slowly add half the olive oil. Season with the lime juice, salt, and cayenne pepper. Transfer to a bowl and keep at room temperature.

Slice the scallops in half horizontally and sprinkle them lightly with sea salt. Heat the remaining olive oil in a large nonstick frying pan. When the oil is almost smoking, brown half the scallop slices over high heat for 1 minute per side. Remove to a plate and repeat with remaining scallops, adding oil if needed. Stir any accumulated juices from the frying pan into the watercress purée, and adjust the salt in the purée.

Spread some of the watercress purée into the center of each of 6 warmed dinner plates, and arrange the beans like the spokes of a wheel over the purée. Place 4 scallop halves in a circle on the top and place a dot of the remaining purée on the scallops. Garnish with watercress sprigs.

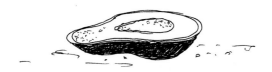

Sea Scallops in Phyllo with Red Cabbage

Working with phyllo dough can be tricky, but the most important rule is to prevent the dough from drying out. That's why you use a damp towel to keep the dough covered and why the sheets are cut in batches.

Makes 6 servings

*1 large red cabbage, tough outer leaves
    and core removed, finely shredded*
3 tablespoons coarse salt
¼ cup safflower oil
1 large shallot, minced
½ cup dry red wine
1 tablespoon Dijon mustard
Pinch of curry powder
2 tablespoons champagne vinegar
*12 large sea scallops of even size, side
    muscles removed*
¼ teaspoon sea salt
10 tablespoons butter
1 package (16 ounces) phyllo dough

Place the cabbage in a large bowl and sprinkle with the salt. Set aside for 2 hours. Add ice cold water to cover, set aside for 30 minutes, drain, and squeeze out excess moisture.

Heat 1 tablespoon of the oil in a small saucepan and cook the shallot over low heat until softened. Add the wine and boil until liquid is reduced to 1 tablespoon. Remove from the heat and make a dressing by whisking in the remaining oil, mustard, curry powder, and champagne vinegar. Blend the dressing with the cabbage and refrigerate until ready to serve.

Sprinkle the scallops with the sea salt. Heat 1 tablespoon of the butter in a large nonstick frying pan, and, when it starts to foam, sauté the scallops for 2 minutes on each side. Remove to a plate.

Preheat oven to 400°F.

Melt the remaining butter. Cut a stack of phyllo dough into 5-inch squares and cover with a damp towel to prevent the dough from drying out. Remove one square and brush its surface with some of the melted butter, starting around the edges. Place a second square on top, and brush it with melted butter. Repeat until you have 4 layers of dough. Place 1 scallop in the center, gather the edges, and pinch the edges together to make a pouch. Repeat with remaining scallops, cutting more phyllo dough as you go along. Brush the pouches with butter, and place them on a nonstick baking sheet. Bake for 20 minutes. Place 2 pouches on each plate and surround with some cabbage. Serve immediately.

Shrimp Toast with Cognac Sauce

Shrimp on little toasts is as elegant as it sounds, but there's another secret to this dish: The toasted French bread absorbs the luscious flavor of the sauce.

Makes 6 servings

4 tablespoons (½ stick) butter
1 large shallot, minced
2 carrots, finely grated
1 cup dry white wine
1 tablespoon tomato purée
1 tablespoon parsley, minced
24 medium shrimp, shelled and deveined
2 tablespoons cognac
1 cup bottled clam juice
1 tablespoon lemon juice
½ cup heavy cream
Salt and freshly ground black pepper to
* taste*
1 French bread baguette
Parsley sprigs, rinsed and dried, for
* garnish*

Preheat oven to 350°F.

Melt 2 tablespoons of the butter in a medium saucepan and cook the shallot and carrots over low heat until softened. Turn up the heat, add the wine, and cook until the liquid is reduced to 1 tablespoon. Remove from the heat and whisk in tomato purée and parsley.

Melt the remaining 2 tablespoons of butter in a large frying pan, and cook the shrimp over high heat for 1 minute per side. Transfer to a plate. Add the cognac to the frying pan, swirl it around, and reduce it to 1 teaspoon. Stir in the clam juice, lemon juice, and cream, and simmer for 15 minutes or until slightly thickened. Add the carrot-shallot mixture and shrimp, and season with salt and pepper.

Remove the ends from the baguette, and cut the bread into 12 slices, each about ½ inch thick. Place the bread on a baking sheet and bake in the preheated oven for 2 minutes.

Place 2 toasted bread slices on each of 6 dinner plates, and top each bread slice with 2 shrimp. Gently reheat the sauce, and spoon it over the shrimp. Serve garnished with the parsley sprigs.

Shrimp Wrapped in Cabbage with Maple Syrup Sauce

Most people probably think of shrimp as an extremely elegant food and cabbage as very humble. Debate it all you want, but the two meet each other in this dish, and the result speaks for itself.

Makes 6 servings

1 large Savoy cabbage
9 strips bacon
*18 extra-large shrimp, peeled and
     deveined*
*3 tablespoons butter, plus additional for
     baking dish and foil*
1 tablespoon maple syrup
1 tablespoon Dijon mustard
½ cup heavy cream
1 tablespoon oyster sauce
1 tablespoon lemon juice
*Salt and freshly ground black pepper to
     taste*
6 mini corn muffins

Discard any tough outer leaves of cabbage. Select 18 large, unblemished leaves, and boil them for 2 minutes in about 3 quarts of salted water. Drain and rinse with cold water. Preheat the oven to 400°F and brush a large baking dish with butter.

Cook the bacon over low heat in a large frying pan until it's translucent and has rendered some of its fat, but the bacon should not be crisp. Drain on paper towels, and cut each strip in half.

Wrap each shrimp with half a bacon strip and set aside. Make a small V-shape cut at the base of each cabbage leaf to remove thick part of stem. Set 1 shrimp on the lower third of each leaf, then fold up the bottom part, fold in the 2 sides, and fold in the top part. Place seam side down in the buttered baking dish, cover the pan with a buttered aluminum foil and bake for 15 minutes.

Melt the 3 tablespoons of butter in a small saucepan, add the maple syrup and mustard, and whisk until smooth. Add the cream and simmer for 15 minutes or until the sauce is slightly thickened. Whisk in the oyster sauce, lemon juice, any drippings from the baking pan, salt and pepper.

Arrange 3 shrimp packages in center of each of 6 warmed dinner plates, spoon some sauce on top, and serve immediately, accompanied by corn muffins.

Snow Peas and Endive with Shiitake Mushrooms

When buying snow peas, select crisp, bright-green pods. This recipe keeps them crunchy by steeping them in boiling water and brightly colored by plunging them in cold water. They pair beautifully with the brown mushrooms and the white endive.

Makes 6 servings

36 fresh shiitake mushrooms with 2-inch caps, stems removed and saved for another use, caps cleaned with damp paper towels
Salt and freshly ground black pepper to taste
2 tablespoons olive oil
1 pound fresh snow peas, ends removed and rinsed
2 Belgian endive
2 inches fresh gingerroot
¼ cup walnut oil
1 tablespoon lime juice
1 tablespoon soy sauce

Lightly sprinkle both sides of the mushroom caps with salt and pepper and drizzle them with the olive oil.

Place the snow peas in about 4 cups of boiling salted water, remove the pot from the heat, and let stand for 5 minutes. Drain the peas and place them in very cold water to set their color. Drain again. Cut the endive in quarters lengthwise and remove the bitter, small triangle at the base of each. Slice into long, thin strips.

Peel and grate the ginger. Squeeze out and reserve the liquid and discard the pulp. Blend the walnut oil, lime juice, soy sauce, and ginger juice with a wire whisk to make a smooth dressing.

Just before serving, heat a nonstick frying pan and brown the mushroom tops over moderate heat for 2 minutes per side. Toss the snow peas and endive with the dressing. Divide among 6 dinner plates, and top with the warm mushroom caps.

Spinach-Bluefish Ravioli

Unlike what you probably envision when you think of ravioli, these are stacks of ingredients, not sealed packets. And they are baked, not boiled. It's the best of both worlds—easy and flavorful.

Makes 6 servings

2 packages (10 ounces each) frozen, chopped spinach
3 tablespoons butter plus additional for baking dish and foil
1 large shallot, minced
12 ounces smoked bluefish, skin removed
2 sheets egg pasta, each about 9 inches square and cut into 3-inch-wide strips
3 tablespoons pine nuts, for garnish
1 cup sour cream
½ cup light cream
1 tablespoon lemon juice
Salt and freshly ground black pepper to taste
Pinch of nutmeg

To make the filling, bring about 3 quarts of salted water to a boil in a large pot, add the frozen spinach, and cook for 10 minutes. Drain and, when cooled, squeeze out excess moisture. Using the same pot, melt the 3 tablespoons of butter and slowly cook the shallot until translucent. Add the spinach, and sauté over low heat for 10 minutes. Place half the spinach mixture and the bluefish in the workbowl of a food processor and blend for 30 seconds. Refrigerate the remaining spinach mixture.

Bring about 4 quarts of salted water to a boil, add the pasta strips to the boiling water 1 at a time to prevent them from sticking, and cook them for 8 minutes. Drain and place the strips in a bowl of cold water.

Preheat oven to 325°F. Grease a large baking dish with butter. Cut a piece of aluminum foil to fit over the pan and brush one side of it with butter.

Cut each pasta strip into 3 squares. Spread 2 tablespoons of filling over one square and top with a second. Spread with 2 more tablespoons of filling and place a third square on top. Repeat with the remaining pasta to make 6 stacks. Place the stacks in the baking dish, cover, buttered side down, with the foil, and bake for 20 minutes.

Place the pine nuts in a nonstick skillet, and brown them lightly over low heat, shaking the pan frequently. Meanwhile, whisk the reserved spinach mixture with the sour cream, light cream, and lemon juice, and simmer for 5 minutes. Season with salt, pepper, and nutmeg.

Place 1 ravioli stack on each of 6 dinner plates, and top each with some of the warm sauce. Sprinkle the pine nuts on top.

Two-Tiered Salad
with Smoked Salmon and Goat Cheese

Besides being just a beautiful presentation, this salad combination also contains my favorite ingredients.

Makes 6 servings

4 large, firm tomatoes, about 3 pounds,
    halved, seeded, and diced
2 tablespoons extra-virgin olive oil
1 clove garlic, put through a garlic press
½ teaspoon salt
Freshly ground black pepper to taste
4 Belgian endive
2 tablespoons walnut oil
2 tablespoons lime juice
Pinch of sugar
6 slices low-salt smoked salmon, about
    ½ pound
Minced dill and basil leaves, for garnish
6 leaves Boston lettuce, rinsed and dried
6 ounces goat cheese, at room
    temperature, cut into 6 portions

Toss the diced tomatoes with the olive oil, garlic, half the salt, and the pepper. Set aside.

Remove any wilted outer leaves from the endive cones, and cut each endive in half lengthwise. Clean with a damp paper towel, and remove a small triangle from the core at the base and discard. Cut lengthwise into very fine strips.

Make a dressing by blending the walnut oil, lime juice, sugar, remaining salt, and freshly ground black pepper to taste.

Just before serving, toss the endive with the dressing, and divide among 6 dinner plates, using just the lower half of each plate. Top each serving with a slice of smoked salmon and garnish with minced dill.

Place a lettuce leaf on the upper half of each plate and place a portion of the diced tomatoes on the leaves. Place a portion of goat cheese on top of the tomatoes, and spoon juice from the tomatoes on top. Garnish with basil leaves.

Vegetable-Salmon Terrine with Tomato Dill Sauce

Don't be put off by the length of this recipe. Terrines can be easy, and you'll be delighted with the presentation. You need heavy-duty oven mitts to maneuver the terrine in and out of the water bath, which helps the terrine cook easily and gently.

Makes 6 servings

1 tablespoon melted butter to prepare loaf
*   pan and wax paper*
1 package (10 ounces) frozen whole-leaf
*   spinach*
1 small cauliflower, stem trimmed and broken
*   into florets*
2 tablespoons cornstarch
1 extra-large egg
1 extra-large egg yolk
¼ teaspoon salt
1 tail-end filet of salmon, about 8 ounces,
*   skin removed*
6 tablespoons sour cream
Pinch of nutmeg
¼ teaspoon salt
1 teaspoon lemon juice
¼ teaspoon sea salt
Tomato Dill Sauce (recipe follows)
Dill sprigs, for garnish

Brush some melted butter on the surfaces of an 8 x 4 x 2½-inch loaf pan. Line the bottom and sides with wax paper and brush the wax paper with some melted butter. Trim any excess paper. Heat about 4 cups of water to use for poaching the terrine.

Bring about 3 quarts of salted water to a boil in a large pot, add the frozen spinach, and cook for 8 minutes. Drain and reserve spinach. Rinse the pan, bring about 3 quarts of salted water to a boil, and add cauliflower florets. Return to the boil and cook for 8 minutes. Drain the cauliflower, cool, and transfer to the workbowl of a food processor. Purée with

cornstarch, egg, egg yolk, and salt for 1 minute, scrape down the sides of the bowl, and process until smooth.

Spread a ¾-inch layer of cauliflower purée into the prepared loaf pan, and smooth the surface with a spatula. Transfer the remaining cauliflower to a bowl, and reserve.

Preheat oven to 375°F.

Squeeze excess moisture from the spinach and place it in the clean workbowl of a food processor. Purée with the sour cream, nutmeg, and salt for about 1 minute, scrape down the sides of the bowl, and process until smooth. Spread half the spinach mixture over the cauliflower mixture, and smooth the surface with a spatula.

Using tweezers, remove any bones remaining in the salmon filet. Cut down the middle along the indentation, and sprinkle both sides with the lemon juice and sea salt.

Place the salmon on top, trimming to make a layer of even thickness. Add the remaining spinach purée, and smooth the surface. Add the remaining cauliflower purée, and smooth the surface. Set the loaf pan into an 11 x 13-inch baking dish and fill pan with the hot water about halfway up the sides of the terrine. Poach the terrine in the oven for 50 minutes, then let cool for 2 hours. Invert the terrine on a cutting board, cover with clear plastic wrap, and refrigerate for at least 4 hours before cutting.

Slice the terrine into 1-inch portions. Line 6 dinner plates with some sauce, and top the sauce with a slice of terrine. Garnish with dill sprigs, and pass the remaining sauce at the table.

Tomato-Dill Sauce

1 large egg
1 large egg yolk
⅔ cup safflower oil
1 tablespoon minced hot chili pepper,
  seeds removed
1 bunch fresh dill, stems removed, to yield
  about 1 cup, rinsed and dried
Pinch of sugar
½ teaspoon salt
2 tablespoons red wine vinegar
1 large tomato, about ½ pound

Make a mayonnaise by placing the egg and the egg yolk in the workbowl of a food processor and, with the machine running, add the oil in a thin stream. Add the chili, dill, sugar, salt, and vinegar, and process until the dill is chopped finely.

Cut the tomato in half horizontally, Remove the seeds, squeeze to extract as much moisture as possible, and cut into 8 pieces. Add the tomatoes to the mayonnaise and pulse until the tomato is cut into small bits. Refrigerate until serving time, and use as directed in previous recipe.

Grains

I haven't forgotten the vegetarians of the world. If you are a vegetarian, this chapter is for you, because most of the recipes in it are a vegetarian's delight. But if you're not, you may not have noticed that today's meatless dishes are heartier than ever, with colors, textures, and ingredients that you'd probably love.

Rice, wheat, potatoes, and beans play a large part in the preparation of my meals. If dishes are prepared with vegetables, beans, or lentils or if any of those ingredients are combined with exotic spices, they can be served as a separate course following an appetizer. When I combine rice with vegetables, I give careful attention to color. And if I think texture is important, I mix pistachio nuts or almonds into the rice or barley. I favor thin, fresh pasta to accentuate the subtle flavor of the spinach lasagna or the fettuccine with salmon butter. But dried pasta containing semolina seems to work best in pasta salads.

Acorn Squash with Bulgur Wheat Filling

If you're looking to put a vegetarian dish on the dinner table, consider appearance and taste. This one is sure to be a hit because of its garam masala, where most of the flavor comes from. It usually contains coriander, cinnamon, caraway, cloves, ginger, nutmeg and peppercorns.

Makes 6 servings

3 small acorn squash
2 tablespoons melted butter, plus some to prepare the baking dish and foil
Salt and freshly ground black pepper to taste
2 tablespoons light brown sugar

Filling:
1 cup coarse bulgur wheat
4 tablespoons butter
½ cup peanuts with their papery skins, coarsely chopped
2 tablespoons poppy seeds
1 tablespoon roasted sesame seeds
1 teaspoon ground cardamom
1 teaspoon ground garam masala (available in Asian markets)
½ teaspoon cayenne pepper

Preheat oven to 400°F. Butter a large baking dish and one side of a sheet of aluminum foil large enough to cover the baking dish.

Clean the squash under cold running water, cut in half horizontally, remove seeds, and cut a thin sliver from the bottom of each half to keep it from rolling. Place in a large buttered baking dish and pour about 1 cup of water around the squash halves. Drizzle the squash with the melted butter, and season lightly with salt and pepper. Sprinkle the brown sugar evenly into the cavities and on the rims, and bake for 35 minutes or until squash is soft when pierced with the tip of a knife.

Reduce oven temperature to 375°F.

Bring about 1½ cups of salted water to a boil in a large saucepan, add the bulgur, stir and bring to a boil. Turn off the heat, cover the pan and let stand for 15 minutes. Drain and fluff with a fork.

Melt the 2 tablespoons of butter in a large frying pan and stir in the peanuts, poppy seeds, and sesame seeds. Add the cooked bulgur, stir to coat with the butter, sprinkle with the ground cardamom, garam masala, and cayenne pepper, and cook over low heat, stirring constantly, for 5 minutes.

Divide the filling among the squash halves, and place the remaining butter, cut in small pieces on top. Cover with the aluminum foil, and heat thoroughly in the oven for about 15 minutes.

Appaloosa Beans with Avocado Topping

The Appaloosa beans in this recipe get their name from the saddle horse native to the northwestern United States. Both are spotted. You could substitute black or pinto beans, but the Appaloosa beans are more attractive in a salad such as this one. Remember, add salt only for the last 5 minutes of cooking, because beans take longer to cook once salt has been added.

Makes 6 servings

1 cup dried Appaloosa beans
1 tablespoon salt
1 pound very ripe tomatoes, skin and
     seeds removed, cut in small dice
6 tablespoons olive oil
2 cloves garlic, peeled
4 large fresh sage leaves, minced
2 tablespoons cider vinegar
3 tablespoons lemon juice
Additional salt and freshly ground black
     pepper to taste
1 very ripe avocado
1 tablespoon freshly squeezed lime juice
1 small onion, minced
3 drops Tabasco
1 cup cilantro, tough stems removed,
     rinsed, and minced
Corn chips

Pick through the beans, discarding any debris, soak them overnight in cold water, and drain.

Place the drained beans in about 2 quarts of boiling water, and cook for 20 to 30 minutes. (Cooking time depends on the beans, so check them frequently. When finished, they should be tender but still firm.) Add the 1 tablespoon of salt for the last 5 minutes of cooking. Drain the beans, rinse them with cold water, and place them in a large mixing bowl. Add all but ½ cup of the diced tomatoes to the beans.

Heat 1 tablespoon of the olive oil in a small frying pan, add the garlic cloves, and brown them all around over medium heat for 10 minutes. Add the minced sage leaves and cook 5 minutes more, stirring constantly. Add the contents of the pan to the beans. Blend the remaining olive oil, vinegar, lemon juice, salt, and pepper, and pour over the beans. Marinate for 4 hours at room temperature or overnight in the refrigerator. Stir occasionally.

Remove the garlic, and, if you marinated in the refrigerator, bring the mixture to room temperature before serving (about 4 hours).

To make the topping, cut the avocado in half, remove the pit, and, with a spoon, remove the flesh. Sprinkle it immediately with the lime juice, and mash it with a fork. Mix with the onion, remaining diced tomatoes, Tabasco, and cilantro. Taste and add salt if necessary. Divide the beans among 6 serving plates, top with the avocado mixture, and serve immediately, surrounded by the corn chips.

Barley Risotto with Basil and Tomatoes

Risotto has become so popular in recent years that adapting it for different grains can multiply the possibilities. Here, common ingredients lead to an uncommonly good dish.

Makes 6 servings

*1 cup pearl barley, picked through and
    rinsed*
2 tablespoons olive oil
1 small onion, minced
*1½ cups Vegetable Stock (page 164) or
    canned chicken broth*
1 large tomato, peeled, seeded, and diced
2 cloves garlic, minced
1 tablespoon butter, softened
*Salt and freshly ground black pepper to
    taste*
*1 cup tightly packed basil leaves, rinsed,
    dried, and minced*

Pick through the barley to remove any debris, rinse, and soak in cold water for 10 minutes.

Heat the olive oil in a large saucepan, cook the onion over low heat until translucent, and add the rinsed barley, mixing well to coat with the oil. Cook for 2 minutes, turn up the heat, and add the stock. Bring to a boil, stir, reduce heat to a simmer, cover pan, and cook for 10 minutes. Stir in the diced tomato and garlic, and simmer, covered, for 15 minutes more.

Blend the butter into the warm barley, season with the salt and pepper, stir in the basil, and serve immediately.

Basmati Rice
with Cardamom Seeds and Garam Masala

Here is more proof of how varied and flavorful a vegetarian dish can be. Many cooks use basmati as their favored rice variety. The intense aroma of the tiny inner seeds of the cardamom pod elevates this rice dish to new culinary heights. If you want to remove the seeds after cooking, tie them in a piece of cheesecloth.

Makes 6 servings

1½ cups basmati rice
1 quart lightly salted water
10 cardamom pods or ½ teaspoon ground
    cardamom
4 tablespoons (½ stick) butter
½ cup salted peanuts with their papery
    skins, coarsely chopped
1 tablespoon garam masala (available in
    Asian markets)
½ teaspoon grated lemon zest
2 tablespoons lemon juice

Soak the rice, covered with cold water, for about 30 minutes, drain, and rinse with cold water. In a large saucepan, bring the quart of salted water to a boil, stir in the rice, return the water to the boil, and cook for 4 minutes. Drain, rinse with cold water, and spread on a large cookie sheet. Set aside, uncovered.

If you're using cardamom pods, crush the pods with the flat side of a knife, remove the small seeds, and discard the shells. Melt the butter in a wok or large frying pan, and add the cardamom seeds or, if you are using it, the ground cardamom. Add the chopped peanuts, and cook for 5 minutes, stirring constantly to coat the peanuts with the butter. Stir in the rice and sprinkle with garam masala, lemon zest, and lemon juice. Stir-fry the rice for 10 minutes over medium heat. Adjust salt and serve immediately or at room temperature.

Black Beans with Tomatillos

Stuffed anything makes an appealing meal. In this recipe, tomato "shells" do the job by holding a filling of contrasting color and exotic taste.

Makes 6 servings

1 cup dried black beans, debris removed, covered with cold water, and soaked overnight
1 tablespoon salt
3 medium tomatoes
Salt
½ pound tomatillos (Mexican green tomatoes), papery outer skins removed
1 clove garlic
1 jalapeño pepper, seeds removed
¼ cup olive oil
2 tablespoons lime juice
1 teaspoon salt
1 bunch fresh mint, small clusters of leaves from the top set aside for garnish, leaves chopped
Salt and freshly ground pepper to taste

Drain and rinse the beans with cold water. Place them in a medium saucepan and add about 4 cups of cold water. Bring to a boil, reduce heat, and cook for 20 minutes or until tender but still firm. Add the 1 tablespoon salt and cook for 5 more minutes. Drain.

Cut the tomatoes in half horizontally, and scoop out the pulp and seeds to make each half into a container. Sprinkle each half with a pinch of salt, and place upside down on paper towels. Plunge the tomatillos into boiling water for 30 seconds. Place them with the garlic and jalapeño in the workbowl of the food processor, purée to a saucelike consistency, add the olive oil, lime juice and 1 teaspoon of salt, blend briefly, and mix with the beans. Add the chopped mint, adjust salt, and add black pepper. Marinate in the refrigerator for 4 hours.

Just before serving, scoop the beans into the tomato "shells" and serve garnished with the reserved mint leaves.

Bulgur Vegetable Pilaf

A hefty addition of chili powder gives this dish some zest, and the generous quantity of beans makes it a substantial meal. And with all that, it's fast, economical, and easy.

Makes 8 servings

2 tablespoons olive oil
1 medium onion, chopped
1 can (28 ounces) crushed tomatoes
2 large cloves garlic, minced
5 tablespoons chili powder
1 teaspoon ground cumin
1 teaspoon dried, crumbled basil
4 stalks celery, rinsed, halved lengthwise, and cut in ⅛-inch pieces
4 medium carrots, peeled, halved lengthwise, and cut in ⅛-inch pieces
2 yellow bell peppers, rinsed, stemmed, seeded, and cut in ½-inch dice
2 red bell peppers, rinsed, stemmed, and seeded, and cut in ½-inch dice
1 cup coarse bulgur wheat, rinsed
1 cup Chicken Stock (page 155) or canned chicken broth
1 can (19 ounces) garbanzo beans, drained and rinsed

2 cans (14 ounces) kidney beans, drained and rinsed
1½ teaspoons salt
1 tablespoon fresh lemon juice
½ pound Monterey Jack cheese, grated

Heat the olive oil in a large Dutch oven on the stovetop, add the onion, and cook over low heat until softened. Add the crushed tomatoes, garlic, chili powder, cumin, and basil, and cook for 5 minutes over low heat. Stir in the celery, carrots, and peppers, and cook while stirring over medium heat for 5 minutes more.

Mix in the bulgur, stock, and beans, simmer for 5 minutes, stirring occasionally, turn off the heat, and stir in the salt and lemon juice. Let stand for 30 minutes to allow the bulgur to absorb the liquid.

Divide between 2 ovenproof serving dishes, each about 8 x 10 inches, and sprinkle evenly with the cheese. Just before serving, preheat oven to 375°F, bake for 15 minutes, and serve.

Cornmeal Gratin
with Fontina Cheese and Tomatoes

This hearty dish is a crowd pleaser. It's a great dish for a party, because you can prepare it hours in advance and bake it at the last minute.

Makes 6 servings

Butter to prepare baking dish
4 cups water
½ teaspoon salt
Pinch of nutmeg
1 cup yellow cornmeal (instant polenta)
Pinch of salt
3 egg whites
1 large tomato, cut into 6 slices, each
*   about ¼ inch thick, seeds removed*
¼ pound Fontina cheese, grated
Leaves of 1 sprig fresh thyme
Coarsely ground black pepper to taste

Butter a 9 x 13-inch ovenproof baking dish.

Bring the water, salt, and nutmeg to a boil in a Dutch oven on the stovetop. Add the cornmeal in a slow, steady stream, mixing constantly with a wire whisk to avoid lumps. With the heat at the lowest possible setting, cook the cornmeal for 10 minutes, stirring occasionally, and transfer to a mixing bowl.

Add the pinch of salt to the egg whites, beat until frothy, fold the egg whites into the still warm cornmeal, and spread evenly into the baking dish. Smooth surface with a spatula dipped in cold water.

Preheat oven to 375°F.

Top the cornmeal with the tomato slices and grated cheese. Sprinkle with thyme leaves and a generous amount of black pepper. Bake until the top is golden brown, about 20 minutes. Cut into 6 portions and serve hot.

Cornmeal Hearts with Maple Glazed Onions

Although these cornmeal hearts will look intricate, they are easy to make and will give a magical look to their neighbors on the plate. Of course, you can cut them into any shape you like, using any cookie cutter.

Makes 6 servings

1 tablespoon butter, plus some to butter the baking dish
4 cups Vegetable Stock (page 164) or canned chicken broth
1 cup yellow cornmeal (instant polenta)
½ cup heavy cream
2 large onions, sliced into ⅛-inch-thick rings
2 tablespoons sherry vinegar
3 tablespoons maple syrup
¼ teaspoon salt
Freshly ground black pepper to taste

Butter a 9 x 13-inch baking dish.

Bring the Vegetable Stock to a boil in a Dutch oven on the stovetop. Add the cornmeal in a slow, steady stream, stirring vigorously and constantly with a wire whisk. Reduce the heat and cook for 10 minutes, stirring occasionally. Transfer to a large mixing bowl.

Whip the cream until the peaks no longer collapse after they're formed. Fold into the still-warm cornmeal, and spread into the buttered baking dish. Smooth the surface using a spatula dipped in cold water, cover with clear wrap, and refrigerate.

Clean the Dutch oven and, on the stovetop, melt the 1 tablespoon of butter. Add the onion rings, cover, and cook over very low heat for 12 minutes. Remove the lid, turn up the heat, and add the vinegar, maple syrup, salt, and pepper. Blend and cook until the liquid has evaporated and the onions are light brown. Set aside.

Preheat oven to 375°F.

Invert the dish with the cornmeal onto a flat surface and, with a cookie cutter or cardboard template, cut out 12 heart-shaped portions. Return the hearts to the baking dish. Top with the glazed onions and bake for 10 minutes. Serve immediately.

Crabmeat Risotto

This recipe can only help risotto move from the restaurant to the home. One reason is that it needs far less attention than the traditional risotto. It's made with basmati rice, and the addition of crabmeat makes it a one-dish meal.

Makes 6 servings

3 cups water
½ teaspoon salt
1 cup white basmati rice, soaked in cold water for 30 minutes
2 tablespoons peanut oil
1 clove garlic, minced
8 ounces backfin crabmeat, picked through
⅛ teaspoon salt
1 tablespoon lemongrass, minced
½ teaspoon cayenne pepper

2 tablespoons soy sauce
2 bunches scallions, roots trimmed and all but 2 inches of green discarded, minced

Bring the water and salt to a boil in a small saucepan. Add the rice, cover, and simmer for 10 minutes. Drain and spread the rice on a large cookie sheet.

Preheat oven to 325°F.

Heat the peanut oil in a Dutch oven on the stovetop. Add the garlic, crabmeat, and salt, and cook, covered, for 5 minutes. Blend in the rice, lemongrass, cayenne pepper, and soy sauce, and place the minced scallions on top. Bake, uncovered, for 15 minutes. Fluff the rice with a fork before serving.

Curried Rice with Red Lentils

Sometimes only the fresh version of an ingredient will work. So it is with the fresh lima beans in this recipe. Use fresh peas as a substitute, but if you can't find them fresh, just omit.

Makes 6 servings

1 cup white basmati rice
2 tablespoons safflower oil
2 cloves garlic, minced
2 tablespoons curry powder (Madras)
1¾ cups Chicken Stock (page 155) or
    canned chicken broth
Butter to prepare baking dish
¾ cup red lentils, picked through and
    rinsed
1 cup freshly shelled lima beans or sweet
    peas
2 tablespoons olive oil
2 tablespoons fresh lemon juice
8 ounces thick, plain yogurt
1 cup fresh mint leaves, minced
Salt and freshly ground black pepper to
    taste

Soak the rice in cold water for 30 minutes, rinse in several batches of cold water, and drain. Heat the safflower oil in a large saucepan, and cook the garlic and curry powder over low heat until a strong curry fragrance starts to rise from pan. Add the rice and stir to coat with the curry powder. Add the stock, bring to a boil, reduce heat, cover, and simmer for 8 minutes. Transfer to a buttered 9 x 13-inch baking dish.

Preheat oven to 275°F.

Rinse the saucepan, bring about 4 cups of salted water to a boil, add the lentils, and cook over low heat for 10 minutes. Drain the lentils, rinse them with cold water, and blend them into the rice. Using same saucepan, again bring about 4 cups of salted water to a boil, add the fresh lima beans, and cook for 3 minutes. Drain, rinse, and stir into the rice. Combine the olive oil and lemon juice, mix into the rice, cover with aluminum foil, and bake for 30 minutes. Whisk the yogurt until smooth, and stir in the mint, salt, and pepper.

Serve directly from the oven or at room temperature. Pass the yogurt mixture on the side.

Individual Spinach Lasagna

Spinach cries out for complementary flavors, and this recipe answers the call nicely. I usually use fresh spinach, but this is a recipe that will work just fine with frozen spinach.

Makes 6 servings

2 packages (10 ounces each) frozen, chopped spinach
6 tablespoons butter, plus some to prepare the baking dish and foil
2 cloves garlic, minced
Salt and freshly ground black pepper to taste
8 ounces sour cream
4 ounces goat cheese, such as Montrachet, crumbled
¼ teaspoon nutmeg
3 tablespoons toasted pine nuts
2 or 3 sheets fresh pasta, cut into 6 strips, each measuring about 3 x 12 inches
6 tablespoons grated Parmesan cheese

Cover the frozen spinach with water in a large saucepan, bring to a boil, reduce heat, and cook for 10 minutes. Drain spinach, let cool, and squeeze out excess moisture. Melt half the butter in a medium saucepan, sauté the garlic until softened, add the spinach, salt, and pepper, and cook for 10 minutes, stirring occasionally. Blend in the sour cream, goat cheese, and nutmeg.

Brown the pine nuts over moderate heat in a nonstick frying pan, shaking the pan frequently to brown evenly. Place on paper towels.

Bring about 6 quarts of salted water to a boil in a large pot, and add the pasta strips 1 at a time to prevent them from sticking and to keep the water at a boil. Stir constantly. Drain the pasta after 2 to 3 minutes (actual cooking time depends on the thickness of the pasta) and rinse with cold water.

Preheat oven to 375°F.

Butter a 9 x 13-inch baking dish. Place a pasta strip on a work surface with the long side toward you. Visualize the pasta strip in 3 parts. Spread 2 tablespoons of the spinach mixture on the first third of the strip, fold the pasta over to cover the spinach, spread another 2 tablespoons of spinach on the pasta and cover that with the last third. Repeat with remaining pasta strips and spinach to make 6 stacks, each with 2 layers of spinach and 3 layers of pasta.

Sprinkle each stack with 1 tablespoon of grated Parmesan cheese. Melt the remaining butter, and drizzle over the top. Cover with the buttered aluminum foil, bake for 15 minutes, remove from the oven, and serve immediately with the pine nuts sprinkled on top.

Kashi with Crisp Prosciutto and Sage

This dish, with the sage, fried prosciutto, and walnut oil—uses assertive flavors, but the chewy texture of the kashi, which is a blend of whole grains, is also significant.

Makes 6 servings

1 cup kashi
3 tablespoons walnut oil
3 tablespoons lemon juice
Salt and freshly ground black pepper to
*   taste*
3 tablespoons Clarified Butter (page 156)
¼ pound sliced prosciutto, shredded
30 fresh small sage leaves
Boston or Bibb lettuce leaves, rinsed and
*   dried*

Cook the kashi in about 2 cups of simmering salted water in a covered 2-quart saucepan for 25 minutes. Set aside, covered, for 5 minutes. Drain, cover with cold water, and drain again. Whisk together the walnut oil and lemon juice, add salt and pepper, and blend into the kashi. Marinate at room temperature for 2 hours.

Melt 1 tablespoon of the clarified butter in a large frying pan, add the prosciutto, and stir over medium heat until the ham is crisp. Drain on paper towels and wipe the frying pan with paper towels.

Shake the sage leaves and tap them on the kitchen counter, but do not wash them. Just before serving, melt the remaining 2 tablespoons of butter in the frying pan, add the sage leaves in one layer, sprinkle with about ¼ teaspoon of salt, and fry until crisp.

Arrange the kashi on lettuce leaves and top with prosciutto and sage leaves. Serve immediately.

Mini-Dumplings with Poppy Seeds

Cooking poppy seeds in butter brings out their unparalleled flavor and sweetness. The blue-gray seed goes beautifully with the dumplings, making this dish very special. Spaetzle-makers are available in cookware shops or through mail-order.

Makes 6 servings

2 cups all-purpose flour
¼ cup grated Parmesan cheese
3 extra-large eggs
¾ cup plus 2 tablespoons cold water
1 teaspoon salt
4 tablespoons (½ stick) butter plus some
*   to prepare baking dish*
1 tablespoon poppy seeds, covered with
*   cold water and soaked for 3 hours*
¼ pound Monterey Jack cheese, grated
*   (optional)*

Place the flour and grated cheese in a mixing bowl, and make a well in the center. Whisk together the eggs, water, and salt, and pour the mixture into the well.

Gradually stir the flour toward the well, blending it to make a smooth, glossy, thick batter. Set aside for 30 minutes.

In a large saucepan, bring about 3 quarts of salted water to a boil. Pour the batter in the container of a spaetzle-maker. Slide the container back and forth so the dumplings will drop into the boiling water, and cook the dumplings for 3 minutes (the dumplings rise to the surface when cooked). Drain the dumplings, and place them in a buttered 9 x 13-inch baking dish.

Preheat oven to 400°F.

Melt the butter, drain the poppy seeds, and stir them in the butter. Cook for 3 minutes, pour the seeds over the dumplings, and mix to coat. Sprinkle with the grated cheese, if you're using it, bake for 15 minutes, stir the dumplings with a spatula, and bake 15 minutes more or until golden. Serve immediately.

Orange-Flavored Rice

Shelled pistachios are wonderful in combination with the other ingredients in this rice dish, but they turn rancid quickly, so I recommend that you shell them yourself. This dish can be prepared hours ahead and makes a beautiful presentation as part of a buffet.

Makes 6 servings

2 cups basmati rice
3 quarts water
2 tablespoons salt
Zest and juice of 2 oranges (½ cup juice
    and zest cut in julienne)
Zest and juice of 1 lemon (¼ cup juice
    and zest cut in julienne)
2 tablespoons pine nuts, toasted
3 tablespoons butter
½ teaspoon curry powder (Madras)
¼ teaspoon saffron threads softened in
    1 tablespoon cold water
3 tablespoons shelled pistachios, chopped
¼ cup fresh parsley, minced
¼ cup fresh chives, minced
Salt and freshly ground black pepper to
    taste

Rinse and cover the rice with cold water, soak for 30 minutes, and drain. Bring the water and salt to a boil in a large saucepan. Add the rice, cook for 4 minutes, drain, and spread on a cookie sheet.

Cook the orange and lemon zests in about 1 quart of boiling water for 1 minute to remove their bitterness. Drain, rinse with cold water, and set aside on paper towels.

Lightly brown the pine nuts in a nonstick frying pan over the lowest possible heat, shaking the pan frequently. Transfer to paper towels.

Melt the butter in a wok or a frying pan with high sides, add the curry powder, and stir to blend. Add the rice, saffron threads and their soaking liquid, pistachios, and pine nuts. Turn up the heat, pour the lemon and orange juices on top, and simmer for 8 minutes, stirring occasionally. Stir in the parsley, chives, orange and lemon zests, salt, and pepper, and serve hot or at room temperature.

Pasta with Almond Parsley Dressing

Traditional pesto uses fresh basil, which is not always available. Changing the herb and the nuts can make a most interesting pasta sauce. This one, using flat-leaf parsley and almonds, is especially pretty.

Makes 6 servings

18 cherry tomatoes
¼ teaspoon salt
2 cups tightly packed flat-leaf parsley, stems removed, rinsed and dried
⅔ cup whole almonds
6 anchovy filets, drained
2 cloves garlic
¼ cup olive oil
Juice of 1½ lemons (about ¼ cup)
½ cup cold water
Salt and freshly ground black pepper to taste
12 ounces egg linguini made with semolina flour
½ pound Monterey Jack cheese, grated

Rinse the cherry tomatoes, cut in half horizontally, scoop out the seeds, sprinkle with the salt, and invert on paper towels to drain. Refrigerate.

Place the parsley, almonds, anchovy filets, and garlic in the workbowl of a food processor, and chop until the almonds are about halfway broken. At that point, slowly add the olive oil to the workbowl in a thin stream, and process until the mixture has become a paste. Set aside ¼ cup for garnish. Add the lemon juice and cold water to the processor bowl. Blend, season with the salt and pepper, and transfer the dressing to a large mixing bowl.

Bring about 4 quarts of salted water to a boil, add the pasta, stir, return the water to a boil, and cook the pasta for 5 minutes or until tender but still firm. Drain, rinse with cold water, and mix immediately with the parsley dressing and the grated cheese.

Using a small spoon, top the cherry tomatoes with the reserved parsley mixture. Arrange the pasta on a large serving platter and surround it with the cherry tomatoes. Serve at room temperature.

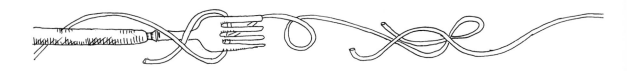

Pasta with Scallion Dressing

Pasta sauces don't have to have an Italian heritage these days. The whole-wheat linguini in this recipe holds up to the Asian-flavored dressing.

Makes 6 servings

¼ cup dark sesame oil
¼ cup soy sauce
½ teaspoon Tabasco sauce
1 tablespoon minced ginger (from a
*   1-inch piece)*
1 large clove garlic, minced
¼ cup toasted sesame seeds
14 ounces fresh whole-wheat linguini
2 large carrots, peeled and cut into
*   julienne*
2 bunches scallions, trimmed, only the
*   white part plus 3 inches of greens,*
*   minced*
½ cup hot Chicken Stock (page 155) or
*   canned chicken broth*

Blend the sesame oil, soy sauce, Tabasco, ginger, and garlic. Set aside.

Toast the sesame seeds in a nonstick frying pan over low heat, tossing frequently until they are light brown and fragrant. Transfer to paper towels.

Bring about 4 quarts of salted water to a boil, add the pasta, stir, return the water to a boil, and cook the pasta for 3 minutes or until tender but still firm. Drain, rinse briefly with cold water, and toss with the carrots and scallions. Strain the dressing and pour it over the pasta.

Just before serving, heat the Chicken Stock and add it to the pasta-vegetable mix. Sprinkle the sesame seeds on top, and serve at room temperature.

Potatoes with Pistachio Filling

The humble potato has an affinity for so many ingredients that with only a bit of extra effort, it can become a regal side dish. Since the potatoes have to be hollowed out, select the ones that are about 1½ inches wide when standing upright.

Makes 6 servings

18 small red potatoes
¼ pound freshly shelled pistachios
1 clove garlic
6 tablespoons olive oil
¼ cup half and half
2 tablespoons grated Parmesan cheese
2 tablespoons lemon juice
Salt and freshly ground black pepper to
*   taste*
Butter to prepare baking dish
2 tablespoons minced parsley

Rinse the potatoes under cold running water, place in a large saucepan, and cover with salted water. Boil until tender, about 10 to 15 minutes, and drain.

Place the pistachios without oil in a nonstick frying pan, set the pan over medium heat, and gently roast the pistachios by stirring and shaking the pan for about 8 minutes. Transfer the nuts to the workbowl of a food processor, and grind with the garlic for 30 seconds. Add ¼ cup of the olive oil in a thin stream, then add the half-and-half. You'll have a paste. Transfer the paste to a mixing bowl and stir in Parmesan cheese, lemon juice, salt, and pepper.

Preheat the oven to 375°F and butter a 9 x 13-inch baking dish.

Cut a thin slice off one end of each potato to allow the potatoes to stand upright. Slice off the opposite end and, using a corer and a rotating motion, hollow out the center of each potato, leaving a ¼-inch shell. Place the remaining 2 tablespoons of olive oil in a small dish and roll the potatoes in it. Place them open side up in the baking dish, sprinkle inside lightly with additional salt and pepper, and stuff the potatoes with the pistachio mixture.

Bake for 15 minutes. Serve garnished with the parsley.

Red Lentils with Bacon and Vinegar

This is a great dish to make when you are new to cooking. It's simple but it's also loaded with flavor. Serve it as a main course, accompanied by a green salad and some good bread.

Makes 6 servings, 4 as a main course

1 cup dried red lentils
4 strips bacon
¼ cup finely chopped onion
1 tablespoon Dijon mustard
1 cup Chicken Stock (page 155) or
   canned chicken broth
Salt and freshly ground black pepper to
   taste
2 medium carrots, cut into julienne
2 stalks celery, cut into julienne
1 tablespoon red wine vinegar

Pick through the lentils and discard any debris. Rinse the lentils, cover them with cold water, and soak for 1 hour. Brown the bacon strips until crisp, drain on paper towels, and discard all but 2 tablespoons of the rendered bacon fat.

Cook the onion in the remaining bacon fat until translucent. Add the drained lentils, mustard, and stock, and bring to the boil. Cover, reduce heat, and simmer the lentils for 10 minutes. Season with salt and pepper, stir in the julienned carrots and celery, and cook for 5 minutes more. Transfer immediately to a serving dish and stir in the vinegar.

Crumble the cooked bacon, and sprinkle the bacon bits on top. Serve at room temperature.

Saffron Risotto with Three Vegetables

This colorful and inexpensive one-dish meal can be prepared ahead and baked briefly just before serving.

Makes 6 servings

¼ cup olive oil
2 cloves garlic, minced
½ cup minced onion
1½ cups risotto rice (arborio)
3 cups Chicken Stock (page 155) or
*   Vegetable Stock (page 164) or*
*   canned chicken broth*
1 teaspoon saffron threads softened in 1
*   tablespoon water*
½ teaspoon grated lemon zest
Salt and freshly ground black pepper to
*   taste*
1 pound fresh spinach, tough stems
*   removed, rinsed*
Pinch of salt
4 tablespoons (½ stick) butter, 2
*   tablespoons melted, 2 tablespoons*
*   left whole*
2 carrots, peeled and cut into sticks
*   ¼ inch thick and 2 inches long*
2 medium zucchini, trimmed, cleaned,
*   and cut into ¼-inch dice*
6 tablespoons Parmesan cheese, coarsely
*   grated*

Heat the olive oil in a large Dutch oven on the stovetop. Add the garlic and onion, and cook over low heat until softened. Add the rice and cook gently for 5 minutes, stirring constantly. Add the stock, the saffron, and the saffron soaking liquid, and bring to a boil. Reduce heat, cover pan, and simmer for 40 minutes, stirring occasionally. Stir in the lemon zest, and season with salt and pepper.

Place the spinach in a large saucepan and add a pinch of salt. Cover the pan and cook over the lowest possible heat for about 5 minutes or until the spinach is wilted. Drain, divide into 6 portions, and form each portion into a ball, squeezing out any excess liquid. Roll the spinach ball in the melted butter and set aside.

Melt the additional butter in a medium saucepan, add the carrots, blend until coated with the butter, and transfer to a plate. Place the zucchini in same saucepan, season with additional salt and pepper, and cook in the butter remaining in the pan for 2 minutes.

Preheat oven to 375°F.

Place the rice in a 9 x 13-inch baking dish, bury the spinach balls evenly in the rice (to define the portions), place the carrot and zucchini on top, sprinkle with the Parmesan, and bake for 15 minutes. Serve immediately.

Spaghetti with Cucumber and Fresh Tarragon

Although this is a year-round dish, it's perfect for summer fare. The toppings feature appealing pastel colors that make for a pasta salad with unusual flavors.

Makes 6 servings

1 seedless cucumber, about 1 pound
¼ teaspoon salt
12 ounces fresh spaghetti or linguini made with semolina flour

Vinaigrette:
¼ cup olive oil
2 tablespoons white wine vinegar
2 tablespoons Dijon mustard
Salt and freshly ground black pepper to taste

Topping:
½ cup pine nuts, toasted
2 hard-cooked eggs, peeled and crumbled
¼ cup Moroccan black olives, pitted and chopped
2 tablespoons capers
Sprigs of fresh tarragon

Peel the cucumber, trim both ends, and, using a vegetable peeler, cut long, thin ribbons of cucumber, discarding any inner seedy core. Place the cucumber strips in a colander, sprinkle with the ¼ teaspoon of salt, and set aside.

To make the vinaigrette, blend the olive oil, vinegar, mustard, salt, and pepper.

Toast the pine nuts over low heat in a dry, nonstick frying pan until the nuts are lightly browned. Combine the pine nuts with the crumbled eggs, chopped olives, capers, and tarragon.

Bring about 4 quarts of salted water to a boil in large pot, add the spaghetti, and cook for 1 to 2 minutes until tender but still firm. Drain, rinse briefly with cold water, and place in a large mixing bowl. Squeeze any excess moisture from the cucumber, and toss it with spaghetti. Add the dressing and mix well. Sprinkle the egg topping over all, and serve at room temperature, garnished with the tarragon sprigs.

Spicy Rice Pilaf

There's no mystery here. An ordinary batch of rice becomes a special side dish with the right mix of flavorings.

Makes 6 servings

1½ cups jasmine rice
2 tablespoons peanut oil
10 cloves
4 bay leaves
1 large shallot, minced
2 cloves garlic, minced
1 tablespoon grated ginger
¼ teaspoon cayenne pepper
⅛ teaspoon ground cinnamon
3 cups Vegetable Stock (page 164) or
    Chicken Stock (page 155) or canned
    chicken broth
2 tablespoons butter

Preheat oven to 350°F. Soak the rice in cold water for 15 minutes, drain, and rinse.

On the stovetop, heat the oil in a Dutch oven. Add the cloves and bay leaves, and cook over low heat until the oil becomes fragrant and the bay leaves are lightly browned, about 10 minutes. Pour the oil through a sieve, or remove the bay leaves and cloves with a slotted spoon and return the oil to the Dutch oven.

Sauté the shallots, garlic, and ginger in the Dutch oven until soft. Stir in the cayenne pepper and cinnamon, add the stock, and bring to a boil. Add the rice, stir briefly, cover the pan, and place the pan in the oven for 10 minutes.

Remove the pan from the oven, stir in the butter, and fluff the rice with a fork. Serve.

Spinach Pasta with Salmon Butter

It's hard to decide whether the colors or the flavors make this such a great dish. So enjoy both. The green of the pasta pairs beautifully with the pink of the salmon butter, and the flavors work in perfect harmony.

Makes 8 servings, 6 as a main course

Zest of 1 lemon, cut into julienne strips
½ pound good-quality smoked salmon, cut in pieces
4 tablespoons (½ stick) butter, softened
1 teaspoon Worcestershire sauce
1 tablespoon tomato paste
¼ teaspoon cayenne pepper
1 clove garlic, put through a garlic press
2 tablespoons lemon juice
Additional salt, depending on the saltiness of the salmon
Romaine lettuce leaves, washed and dried, for garnish
1 ½ pounds fresh spinach pasta (vermicelli or angel-hair)
1 bunch chives, minced

Drop the lemon zest in about 1 quart of boiling water, cook for 1 minute, drain, rinse with cold water, and set aside.

Purée the smoked salmon in the workbowl of a food processor and, with the machine running, add the softened butter. Process until smooth. Keep the salmon butter near the stove so it stays soft. Mix in the Worcestershire, tomato paste, cayenne pepper, garlic, and lemon juice. Season with salt, if necessary.

Roll up the lettuce leaves, and cut into ribbons ⅛ inch wide. Place in a plastic bag and refrigerate.

Bring about 6 quarts of salted water to a boil in a large pot, and cook the pasta for 1 minute. Drain, rinse with hot water, return to the pot, add the salmon butter, lemon zest, and chives, and toss. Divide among preheated plates, and serve garnished with the lettuce ribbons.

Three-Bean Salad with Sun-Dried Tomatoes

For the three beans to retain their distinct colors, I used separate containers to soak and cook each. I used to shop for specialty beans, such as the turtle (black) and adzuki (red) in health-food stores, but lately I've found them in supermarkets as well.

Makes 6 servings

½ cup dried baby lima beans
½ cup dried black turtle beans
½ cup dried red adzuki beans
3 tablespoons safflower oil
1 clove garlic, minced
2 large carrots, peeled and cut into
    julienne
3 stalks celery, cut into julienne
4 large sun-dried tomato halves in oil,
    minced, plus 2 tablespoons oil from
    the tomatoes
¼ cup lemon juice
1 tablespoon cider vinegar
½ teaspoon salt
Freshly ground tellicherry pepper to taste
Baby greens, rinsed and dried

Pick through the beans and pick out any debris, soak the beans for 2 hours, then rinse them. Place each batch in separate saucepans, and add at least 2 quarts of water to each. Bring to a boil and reduce to a simmer. The cooking time for each depends on the type of bean. Start testing for doneness after 20 minutes; the beans should be tender but still firm to the bite. Add 1 teaspoon of salt to each pot for the final 5 minutes of cooking. Drain the beans, rinse with cold water, and place in a mixing bowl.

Heat 1 tablespoon of the safflower oil in a large frying pan, and cook the garlic for 5 minutes, being careful not to brown the garlic. Add the carrots, celery, and sun-dried tomatoes, and stir-fry for 2 minutes. Add to the beans and blend.

Whisk the remaining safflower oil, the oil from the sun-dried tomatoes, the lemon juice and the vinegar, season with the salt and pepper, and toss with the beans and vegetables. Marinate at room temperature for at least 2 hours, stirring occasionally.

Serve on a bed of baby greens.

Two-Colored Rice

Color is so important to food's appeal that it often elevates a common food—rice, for example—to unusual heights. Serve the two rices in this recipe side by side for an unforgettable side dish.

Makes 6 servings

2 tablespoons olive oil
2 cloves garlic, minced
½ cup minced onion
1½ cups risotto rice (arborio)
3 cups Chicken Stock (page 155) or
*   Vegetable Stock (page 164) or*
*   canned chicken broth*
1 large tomato, peeled, seeded, and
*   puréed*
Salt and freshly ground black pepper to
*   taste*
1 package (10 ounces) frozen, chopped
*   spinach*
1 tablespoon butter
1 teaspoon grated lemon zest
¼ cup heavy cream
Gated Parmesan cheese (optional)

Heat the olive oil in a Dutch oven on the stovetop. Cook the garlic and onion over low heat until softened Add the rice, and stir until it is well coated, pour in the stock, and bring to a boil. Reduce to a simmer, cover, and cook for 30 to 40 minutes or until the rice is tender but still firm to the bite.

Place the tomato purée in a small saucepan, heat briefly, season with salt and pepper, and keep warm.

In a medium saucepan, cook the frozen spinach for 10 minutes in about 1 quart of salted boiling water. Drain the spinach, squeezing out any excess moisture. Melt the butter in the saucepan, add the spinach and a pinch of each salt and pepper, cover, and cook over low heat for 5 minutes. Stir in the lemon zest and the cream.

Just before serving, reheat the rice. Blend half of it with the puréed tomatoes and stir the spinach mixture into the rest. Serve the two rices side by side on a serving plate, and pass the grated cheese at the table.

Vegetable Polenta

Polenta is a coarse, yellow corn semolina and is available in specialty stores. For this recipe, yellow cornmeal cannot be substituted because it lacks texture. This is comfort food that will please everyone who eats it. And because it can be made in advance, it will please everyone who makes it, too.

Makes 6 servings

Butter to prepare baking dish
3 tablespoons olive oil
1⅓ cups polenta
3½ cups Chicken Stock (page 155) or
*   canned chicken broth*
2 medium carrots, cut into small dice
2 stalks celery, cut into small dice
Salt and freshly ground black pepper to
*   taste*
¼ pound Monterey Jack cheese, grated
1 bunch scallions, trimmed, white part
*   and 3 inches of greens only, minced*
Mexican Tomato Sauce (page 163,
*   optional)*

Butter an 8-inch square baking dish.

Heat the olive oil in a Dutch oven on the stovetop. Add the polenta and toast it for 2 minutes, stirring constantly with a wooden spoon. Add the stock, simmer for 5 minutes, add the carrots and celery, and cook, stirring occasionally, over low, steady heat for 20 minutes. Season with salt and pepper. Transfer the polenta to the baking dish. This recipe can be prepared ahead of time to this point.

Place an oven rack on the second position from the top, and preheat the broiler.

Sprinkle the grated cheese and scallions on top of the polenta, and broil until the top is golden brown, about 5 minutes. Cut into squares with a metal spatula, and serve, passing the warm tomato sauce separately at the table.

White Corn Grits Soufflé

Grits have gone way beyond their Southern roots, helped by some interesting flavor additions and cooking techniques. These grits are one example. The whipped egg whites make them light and fluffy.

Makes 6 servings

2 cups water
½ teaspoon salt
Pinch of nutmeg
1 cup white corn grits
Butter to prepare baking dish
2 tablespoons grated Parmesan cheese
2 extra-large eggs, separated
½ pound Monterey Jack cheese, grated

Bring the water, salt, and nutmeg to a boil in a Dutch oven on the stovetop.

Using a wire whisk, stir in the grits in a slow stream, reduce the heat to a simmer, and cook for 10 minutes, stirring occasionally to prevent sticking. Transfer to a mixing bowl.

Preheat the oven to 400°F, butter a 7 x 11-inch baking dish, and sprinkle the bottom of the dish with Parmesan cheese.

Beat the egg whites with a pinch of salt until stiff. Whisk the egg yolks and all but 2 tablespoons of the Monterey Jack cheese into the still-warm grits. Fold in the egg whites, and transfer the mixture to a baking dish. Sprinkle with the remaining cheese, and place in the oven. Reduce oven temperature to 375°F, bake for 25 minutes or until the top is golden and the grits are slightly puffed, and serve immediately.

Vegetables

I loved the sign that I saw a few years ago on a tomato bin: "Tomatoes grown by machines should be eaten by machines." Amen, and my thanks to the disgruntled shopper who put the sign there. And what a great example, for who among us has not looked in disgust at one of those pale tennis balls masquerading as a tomato.

The good news is that so much high-quality produce can be obtained year round. It may be an off-season where I live, but somewhere in the world, a tomato is ripening on the vine. The bad news is that the cost is probably horrifying. And regardless of season, there are still days when the quality of some vegetable or salad is just unacceptable.

You, the cook, need to be open-minded. You've got to be willing to switch from one recipe to another when selecting a vegetable dish for your menu. And you've got to spend a little time picking your produce. I handpick all vegetables, and I'll dig deep into the bin to seek out those firm, dark green zucchinis that I plan to fill with quinoa. I also don't hesitate to snap a green bean to verify its crispness and I'll examine every piece of vegetable or fruit before I put it in my shopping basket.

Be just as meticulous once you get it home. I'll barely cook broccoli, green beans, and fennel, so they remain crisp and retain their color. If I have a vegetable in the cabbage family, I'll blanch it briefly to remove some of the strong flavor.

The quantities for these recipes will give you the right amount to accompany dishes from the poultry or grain section. But if you'd like to serve any of these as a main course, just increase the quantities.

Artichoke Bottoms with Shiitake Mushrooms

Talk about great taste combinations. Shiitake mushrooms have an earthy, woodsy taste that's incomparable with the nutty taste of the artichoke. Serve this as an appetizer, or put atop some baby greens for a salad.

Makes 6 servings

6 large artichokes
1 lemon, cut in half
½ cup cider vinegar
⅓ pound fresh shiitake mushrooms,
*   including 6 with perfect 2-inch caps*
4 tablespoons (½ stick) butter, plus
*   additional to prepare the baking dish*
Salt and freshly ground black pepper to
*   taste*
1 large shallot, minced
¼ cup white wine
3 tablespoons pimientos, drained and
*   minced*
2 tablespoons tiny capers, drained

Cut off enough of the artichoke stems to allow easy removal of the first three layers of outer leaves. Rub the cut part of the artichoke with the cut side of a lemon half to prevent discoloration. In a large saucepan, bring about 2 quarts of salted water plus the cider vinegar to a boil and cook the artichokes for 25 minutes. Drain, place upside down on paper towels, and, when cool enough to handle, pull off all the leaves and reserve them for another use. Remove and discard the fuzzy choke.

Wipe the mushrooms clean with paper towels, reserving the 6 perfect caps. Chop the remaining mushrooms and stems. Melt half the butter in a frying pan, and brown the 6 mushroom caps over moderate heat for 3 minutes on each side. Sprinkle lightly with salt and pepper, and set aside. Add the remaining butter to the same frying pan, and cook the minced shallot over low heat until soft. Add the chopped mushrooms and cook for 5 minutes more. Add the wine, and boil until all the liquid has evaporated and the mixture becomes dry and starts to brown. Stir in the pimientos and capers, mix well, and adjust the salt and pepper. Set aside.

Preheat oven to 375°F.

Just before serving, place the mushroom caps in a buttered baking dish and top each with an artichoke bottom. Place the mushroom mixture on top and heat in oven for 5 to 10 minutes.

Belgian Endive with Green Beans and Poppy Seeds

This salad is the perfect combination of color and texture. The endive are delicate while the beans are sturdy. And both benefit from this lemony dressing.

Makes 6 servings

1 pound green beans or haricots verts,
    tips removed and rinsed
¼ cup hazelnut oil
⅛ teaspoon salt
Freshly ground black pepper to taste
1 tablespoon lemon juice
¼ teaspoon grated lemon zest
3 tablespoons toasted poppy seeds, for
    garnish
2 large Belgian endive

Cook the beans in about 5 quarts of boiling salted water for 5 minutes, or until tender. Drain and immediately place the beans in ice-cold water to stop the cooking and set the color. Drain and pat dry with paper towels. Place the beans in a dish, drizzle them with the hazelnut oil, season with salt and pepper, add the lemon juice and lemon zest, and mix.

Toast the poppy seeds in a small nonstick frying pan over very low heat for 2 minutes.

Remove any discolored or blemished outer leaves from the endive, and wipe with damp paper towels. Break off 24 large outer leaves from the cones and place 4 on each plate. Using the endive leaves as containers, divide the beans among them. Spoon some dressing on top, sprinkle with poppy seeds, and serve immediately.

Brussels Sprouts with Peanuts

If you don't like brussels sprouts, it's probably because of their strong and sometimes bitter flavor. Blanching the sprouts in garlic and bay leaf-flavored water will rid them of that taste and make them great carriers for more pleasing flavors, such as garlic and peanuts.

Makes 6 servings

1½ pounds brussels sprouts of even size
4 cloves garlic, peeled
1 bay leaf
2 tablespoons butter
¼ cup Spanish peanuts
1 tablespoon lemon juice
Salt and freshly ground black pepper to
      taste

Wash the sprouts, remove any yellow and wilted outer leaves, and make crosswise incisions into the stems. Cook the garlic cloves and bay leaf for 5 minutes in about 2 quarts of boiling, salted water. Add the sprouts, cook for 10 minutes, drain, and cut sprouts into quarters. Mash the garlic. Melt the butter in a large skillet, add the mashed garlic, sprouts, peanuts, and lemon juice. Toss, and season with salt and pepper.

Cabbage Rolls with Vegetables

Everyone loves wrapped food—especially when the wrapper itself is edible. The curly-leafed Savoy cabbage is more delicate in flavor, and it's easy to wrap around the vegetables. The recipe calls for 2 heads of cabbage because it's the only way to get 12 sufficiently large leaves.

Makes 6 servings

2 large heads Savoy cabbage
2 tablespoons safflower oil
½ pound carrots, peeled and cut in julienne
½ pound zucchini, ends cut off, cleaned and cut in julienne
1 leek, halved lengthwise, washed thoroughly, and cut in julienne
2 stalks celery, trimmed and cut in julienne
2 small cloves garlic, minced
Salt and freshly ground black pepper to taste
Butter to prepare baking dish and aluminum foil
1 cup Vegetable Stock (page 164)
Monterey Jack cheese (optional)

Remove and discard any tough outer leaves from the cabbage. Peel off 6 large leaves from each cabbage, and reserve the rest for another use. Drop the 12 leaves into about 4 quarts of boiling, salted water in a large pot for 2 minutes. Drain, rinse with cold water, and place the leaves on paper towels.

Heat the oil in a wok or a large frying pan and stir-fry the carrots, zucchini, leek, celery, and garlic for 3 minutes. Season with salt and pepper.

Preheat oven to 350°F. Grease a baking pan with the butter.

Place the first cabbage leaf, with the core pointing toward you, on your work surface. Make a small V-shaped incision to cut away the tough tip of the core, and place 2 tablespoons of the vegetable mixture into the middle of the leaf. Fold up the bottom part, then fold in the 2 sides, and close by folding down the top part. Place the rolls, seams down, in a large buttered baking dish, and repeat with the remaining leaves and vegetables.

Pour the stock and accumulated juices from the vegetables over the cabbage, and sprinkle with the grated cheese, if desired. Cover the pan tightly with the buttered aluminum foil and bake for 20 minutes.

Carrots and Turnips with Parsley and Orange

Makes 6 servings

1 pound fresh carrots
1 pound fresh young turnips
Pinch of sugar
½ teaspoon salt
1 bay leaf
4 tablespoons (½ stick) butter
1 cup Italian (flat-leaf) parsley, stems
    removed, rinsed, thoroughly dried,
    and minced
2 tablespoons frozen orange-juice
    concentrate

Peel the carrots and turnips, and cut them into ½-inch-wide and 2-inch-long sticks. Cover the carrots with cold water, add the sugar, bring to a boil, and cook for 1 minute. Drain. Cover the turnips with cold water; add the salt and bay leaf, bring to a boil and cook for 1 minute. Drain and discard the bay leaf.

Melt the butter in a large frying pan, and add the carrots, turnips, and parsley. Stir over low heat until coated with butter, then turn up the heat and add the juice concentrate. Heat thoroughly while swirling the vegetables around.

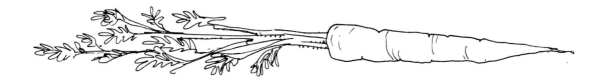

Carrots with Basil Hollandaise

Certainly the carrots are the star of this dish, especially if garden fresh baby carrots are available and you can serve them with a bit of greens left on. Of equal importance is the fresh basil, and if it's not up to snuff or substandard, use fresh chives or flat-leaf parsley instead.

Makes 6 servings

2 pounds fresh baby carrots or 2 bunches
  regular fresh carrots
5 tablespoons butter, 1 tablespoon left
  whole, 4 tablespoons melted
Pinch of sugar
Pinch of salt
¾ cup water
1 extra-large egg yolk
1 tablespoon Dijon mustard
1 tablespoon lemon juice
Salt and freshly ground black pepper to
  taste
1½ cups fresh basil leaves, rinsed and
  dried

If you use baby carrots, leave them whole with about ¼ inch of greens left on. If you use regular carrots, peel them, cut off a small slice from each end, and cut them into pieces ¼ inch wide and 1 inch long.

Melt the 1 tablespoon of whole butter in a large saucepan and toss the carrots in the butter until they are glossy, about 3 minutes. Add the sugar, salt, and ½ cup of the water, cover, and cook for 3 minutes.

Just before serving, make the hollandaise by melting the remaining 4 tablespoons of butter. In a small saucepan, whisk together the egg yolk, mustard, lemon juice, and remaining ¼ cup of water, set the pan over the lowest possible heat, and slowly add the melted butter, stirring vigorously with a wire whisk. Remove from the heat as soon as the sauce starts to thicken, add the salt and pepper, and set aside.

Set aside about a third of the basil leaves for garnish. Chop the rest of the basil, and blend it into the hollandaise.

Drain the carrots, arrange them in a wheel pattern on individual plates, and spoon the hollandaise over. Garnish with the basil leaves.

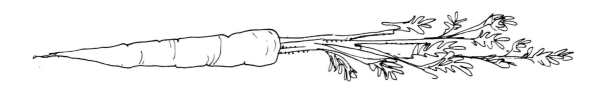

Carrots with Marsala Wine

The better the Marsala, the better this dish. After the alcohol evaporates, you'll be left with a beautiful glaze that will transform plain carrots into a tasty treat.

Makes 6 servings

1 ½ pounds tender young carrots, peeled and cut into sticks ¼ inch thick and 2 inches long
2 tablespoons butter
½ teaspoon sugar

½ cup Marsala wine
Pinch of salt
2 tablespoons lemon juice

Melt the butter in a medium saucepan, add the sugar, and, as soon as the sugar is lightly brown, add the carrots and cook over high heat for 1 minute. Pour the wine on top, add the salt, and bring to a boil. Reduce heat and cook until the wine has evaporated. Remove from the heat, stir in the lemon juice, and serve.

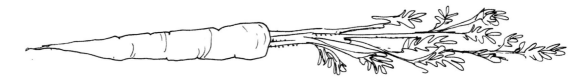

Cauliflower and Broccoli with Ginger Sauce

The flavor here is distinctly Asian, but the trick is in the concentration of two key flavors, ginger and garlic. Grating both accentuates their flavor, and squeezing their juices goes an extra step.

Makes 6 servings

1 small head cauliflower
1 large bunch broccoli, 4 cups florets
½ cup Vegetable Stock (page 164)
1 tablespoon soy sauce
2-inch piece fresh gingerroot, peeled, grated, and squeezed to yield 1 teaspoon juice
1 clove garlic, peeled, grated, and squeezed to yield 1 teaspoon juice
2 tablespoon toasted sesame seeds

Remove the outer leaves from the cauliflower. Break off and rinse individual florets. Cut off broccoli florets to include 2 inches of stem. Rinse, and reserve remaining stems for another use.

Cook the cauliflower florets for 2 minutes in about 4 quarts of salted water brought to a boil in a large saucepan. Remove the cauliflower with a slotted spoon, place into ice-cold water, and drain. Return the water in the saucepan to a boil, cook the broccoli for 1 minute, drain, and place in ice-cold water. Drain.

Combine the Vegetable Stock, soy sauce, and the ginger and garlic juices in a saucepan. Bring to a boil and simmer for 10 minutes. Reduce heat, add the vegetables, heat for 2 minutes, and serve in soup plates, garnished with the toasted sesame seeds.

Collard Green Rolls with Bacon and Pine Nuts

These rolls are a flavor riot, helped by the garam masala, a spice blend that contains cardamom, coriander, black pepper, and fennel flower seeds. Please your vegetarian friends by preparing these rolls without the bacon. There'll still be lots of flavor to go around.

Makes 6 servings

1 large bunch collard greens, about 1½
*   pounds, tough stems removed, rinsed*
¼ cup pine nuts
4 strips bacon or 2 tablespoons olive oil
2 shallots, minced
⅛ teaspoon salt
Freshly ground black pepper
½ cup canned, crushed tomatoes diluted
*   with ½ cup water*
½ teaspoon salt
1 tablespoon garam masala (available in
*   Asian markets)*
Pinch of ground cloves
Butter, for greasing wax paper

Set aside 12 intact leaves from the collard greens. Remove the tough inner ribs from the remaining leaves, roll them up, and cut them into ⅛-inch-wide ribbons.

To make the filling, brown the pine nuts over low heat in a nonstick skillet, shaking the pan frequently so the nuts brown evenly. Transfer the pine nuts to paper towels. Cook the bacon strips, if you are using them, in the same pan until crisp. Drain on paper towels and break into small pieces. Discard all but 2 tablespoons of the bacon fat, or, if you are omitting the bacon, add 2 tablespoons of olive oil. Add the minced shallots and cook over low heat until translucent. Add the chopped collard leaves, the ½ teaspoon of salt, and the black pepper, sauté for 20 minutes, stirring frequently, remove the pan from the heat, and blend in the pine nuts and the bacon bits.

Preheat oven to 350°F.

Place the crushed tomatoes, the ½ teaspoon salt, the garam masala, and the cloves in a Dutch oven, blend well, and bring to a boil on the stovetop. Turn off the heat.

Bring about 3 quarts of salted water to a boil in a large saucepan, and drop the whole collard leaves in. Cook for 2 minutes and drain.

Place the first leaf on a flat surface or cutting board with the stem toward you. Cut out and discard a small triangle from the bottom part of the rib, heap 1 tablespoon of the filling into the center of the leaf, fold in the sides, and roll up. Place seam side down in the Dutch oven. Repeat with the remaining leaves.

Using the lid of the Dutch oven as guide, cut out a piece of wax paper. Butter one side and place, buttered side down, on the vegetable rolls. Place the lid on the pan, and bake for 20 minutes.

Serve 2 rolls per person with the extra sauce spooned on top.

Fennel with Fennel Seeds and Lemon

Fennel is a vegetable with a taste like no other—licorice-like with an appealing crunch. Don't try to match such an assertive flavor. Instead, augment it in a different form—in this case, fennel seeds.

Makes 6 servings

2 large bulbs fennel with tops and ferny
*   leaves*
1 tablespoon lemon juice
2 tablespoons butter, plus additional for
*   baking dish and aluminum foil*
1 tablespoon dried fennel seeds
1 teaspoon grated lemon zest
Freshly ground black pepper

Preheat oven to 375°F.

Cut off finger-like pieces from the fennel bulbs. Reserve the ferny leaves and mince enough of them to measure about ½ cup. Stand the bulbs upright and cut them down the middle. Place them rounded side down and cut each half into 6 wedges.

Bring about 3 quarts of salted water containing the 1 tablespoon of lemon juice to a boil in a large saucepan. Add the fennel, return the water to a boil, and cook for 6 minutes, or until tender. Drain and rinse briefly with cold water.

Grease a large baking dish. Melt the 2 tablespoons of butter in a large saucepan over medium heat. Cook the fennel seeds in the melted butter for 5 minutes, add the cooked fennel and the minced fennel leaves, and blend. Transfer to a baking dish, and sprinkle with the lemon zest and freshly ground black pepper. Lightly brush a piece of aluminum foil with butter and cover the dish, butter side down. Bake for 10 minutes.

Green Beans with Sunflower Seeds and Walnut Oil

It always amazes me how the most common vegetable can come alive by pairing it with a couple of equally common flavorings. You can't go wrong when the additions are seeds or flavored oils.

Makes 6 servings

2 pounds fresh, young green beans, rinsed and tips removed
Zest of 1 orange cut in julienne
1 tablespoon butter
½ cup sunflower seeds
1 tablespoon soy sauce
1 tablespoon frozen orange-juice concentrate
3 tablespoons walnut oil

Place the beans into a large saucepan with about 6 quarts of rapidly boiling salted water, and cook until tender but firm to the bite, about 3 minutes. Drain the beans, and place them in ice-cold water to stop the cooking and set their color. Drain and place on paper towels.

Cook the orange zest for 1 minute in a small saucepan with about 1 quart of boiling water. Drain and rinse with cold water. In a small nonstick frying pan, melt the butter over low heat, and add the sunflower seeds, and cook while stirring occasionally until brown. Transfer the seeds to paper towels.

Blend the soy sauce, orange-juice concentrate, and walnut oil in a large bowl. Toss with the beans and orange zest, and serve with the sunflower seeds sprinkled on top.

Hearts of Palm with Zucchini and Red Peppers

There is a reason I picked this particular vegetable combination. It's because all the vegetables stay crisp, even after several hours of marinating

Makes 6 servings

1 can (14 ounces) hearts of palm
1 pound small zucchini, each about 1
*   inch wide*
¼ cup olive oil
2 tablespoons lemon juice
½ teaspoon salt
Freshly ground black pepper
2 large Roasted Peppers (page 161), cut
*   in thin strips*
1 cup loosely packed basil leaves
6 outer leaves from a head of Boston
*   lettuce, rinsed and dried*

Drain hearts of palm, rinse with cold water, and cut into ¼-inch rounds. Rinse the zucchini under cold water, cut off the ends, slice in half lengthwise, then cut crosswise into ½-inch pieces.

Blend the olive oil, lemon juice, salt, and pepper in a large salad bowl. Add the hearts of palm, zucchini, and strips of Roasted Pepper to the dressing, blend, and marinate for at least 4 hours, tossing them occasionally. Keep refrigerated.

Just before serving, remove the stems from the basil leaves, rinse and dry the leaves, and shred the leaves finely. Blend the basil with the vegetables. Place 1 lettuce leaf in the center of each of 6 plates and, using the leaves as containers, fill them with some of the vegetable salad.

Kale with Olive Oil and Garlic

Stir-frying is a great way to cook lots of food with little additional fat. But you've got to consider the size and texture of each ingredient in order to get even cooking. Kale has a coarse texture and must be shredded very fine.

Makes 6 servings

2 pounds fresh kale, wilted or yellowed
*   leaves discarded*
2 tablespoons extra-virgin olive oil
2 large cloves garlic, thinly sliced
Salt and freshly ground black pepper to
*   taste*
1 tablespoon lemon juice

Cut off the stems of the kale leaves, rinse them individually under cold running water, and cut across into very fine shreds. Heat the olive oil in a wok or a large frying pan, and cook the garlic until medium brown. Add the kale and stir-fry over high heat for 15 minutes. Season with the salt and pepper, transfer the kale to a serving dish, drizzle the lemon juice on top, and toss.

Leek Pastries
with Goat Cheese and Yellow Tomato Sauce

Don't skip this recipe just because you can't find yellow tomatoes. Use red ones. Although they're juicier, compensate by placing the purée in a saucepan and simmering to reduce the liquid.

Makes 6 servings

2 pounds leeks, blemished leaves and roots, and all but 4 inches of dark green removed
¼ pound (1 stick) butter
¼ teaspoon nutmeg
¼ teaspoon salt
1 package (16 ounces) phyllo dough (see note)
4 ounces goat cheese, cut into 6 portions
1 pint yellow cherry tomatoes
1 tablespoon balsamic vinegar
1 tablespoon olive oil
½ teaspoon salt
Freshly ground black pepper to taste

Slice the leeks in half lengthwise and rinse thoroughly under cold running water, spreading the leaves to remove any soil lodged between them. Cut the leeks across into 1-inch-wide pieces to yield about 12 cups. Cook the leek pieces for 3 minutes in about 2 quarts of boiling salted water. Drain and squeeze out excess moisture.

Melt 1 tablespoon of the butter in a large nonstick frying pan, and add the leeks. Season with the nutmeg and salt, blend well, and cook for 2 minutes. Turn off the heat, and divide into 6 portions.

Preheat oven to 375°F.

Melt the remaining butter, unfold the phyllo dough, cut a stack of 8-inch squares, and immediately cover the dough with a damp dish towel to prevent drying.

Working quickly, remove the first phyllo square from the stack, and brush, edges first, with melted butter. Place a second square on top, and brush with butter. Repeat with 3 more squares, place a portion of leeks in the center, and top with a portion of goat cheese. Gather the edges of the dough, and pinch together to make a pouch. Make 5 more pastry pouches. Brush all the finished pouches with melted butter, place them on a baking sheet. (The recipe can be prepared ahead to this point. If so, refrigerate.)

Bake the pastries for 20 minutes.

In a blender or food processor, purée the tomatoes, vinegar, and olive oil until smooth. Pour the mixture through a sieve, pressing on the solids. Season with the salt and pepper.

Spread the center of each of 6 dinner plates with some tomato purée, and top each with a pastry.

Note: Although 1 package is sufficient to make this recipe, I recommend having an extra package on hand in case some of the sheets are so difficult to separate that they must be discarded.

Swiss Chard Gratin

The spinach-like leaves and broad white stalks of the chard require different cooking times. Milk is added to the boiling water to preserve the whiteness of the stalk.

Makes 6 servings

3 bunches Swiss chard, about 3 pounds
½ cup milk
¼ pound thinly sliced ham
½ cup grated Monterey Jack cheese
Butter to prepare the baking dish

Cut along the white stem of the chard and remove the dark green leaves. Rinse the leaves under cold running water, and set them aside. Rinse the stems, and cut them into 1-inch pieces.

Bring about 2 quarts of salted water and the milk to a boil in a large saucepan, add the stem pieces, and simmer for 10 minutes. Add the leaves and simmer for 3 minutes more. Drain and rinse to remove any milk residue, and squeeze out extra moisture from the leaves.

Roll up the ham slices, and cut them into ribbons ⅛ inch thick.

Preheat oven to 375°F.

Butter a large baking dish or 6 individual gratin dishes, and distribute the cooked stem pieces on the bottom of dish. Top with the greens, sprinkle with the grated cheese, and decorate with the ham ribbons. Bake for 30 minutes, or until the cheese has browned and the ham is crispy.

Swiss Chard with Green Hollandaise

This one is for the eyes as well as for the palate. It's easy enough to change the color of a basic hollandaise, and that's what I do here to enhance the presentation.

Makes 6 servings

3 bunches Swiss chard, about 3 pounds
½ cup milk
4 tablespoons (½ stick) butter
2 extra-large egg yolks
1 tablespoon Dijon mustard
1 tablespoon lemon juice
¼ cup cold water
¼ cup hot Chicken Stock (page 155) or
*   canned chicken broth*
Salt and freshly ground black pepper to
*   taste*

Remove the leaves from the Swiss chard by cutting along the center white ribs. Rinse the ribs and cut them into 4-inch pieces. The ribs are fatter at the bottom, so cut the broader ribs in half lengthwise to give you pieces of uniform size. Bring about 4 quarts of salted water and the milk to a boil, and cook the rib pieces in the water for 10 minutes.

Using a slotted spoon, remove the rib pieces, rinse with cold water, and place on paper towels. Return the water to the boil, add the green leaves, cook for 2 minutes, drain, and rinse to remove milky residue. When cooled, squeeze out excess moisture and purée in food processor.

Melt the butter. In a separate small saucepan, whisk together the egg yolks, mustard, lemon juice, and cold water. Set the pan over the lowest possible heat, using a diffuser if necessary. Slowly add the melted butter, stirring continuously with a wire whisk until the sauce has lightly thickened. Remove the saucepan from the heat, and stir in the puréed leaves and the hot stock. Season with salt and pepper and add more stock if the sauce is too thick.

Just before serving, divide the chard ribs among 6 dinner plates. Spoon the sauce over half the stems, leaving other half of the stems white.

Vegetable Ragout

Only two tablespoons of olive oil are used to cook this colorful and healthy dish. Add an extra cup of Vegetable Stock and, voilà, you have a soup.

Makes 6 servings

2 tablespoons olive oil
1 medium onion, cut into thin rings
1 tablespoon sweet paprika
1 medium dill pickle, minced
½ cup dry red wine
1 cup Vegetable Stock (page 164)
1 cup carrots, peeled and cut in ½-inch
*   rounds*
2 cups small red potatoes, cleaned and
*   cut in bite-size pieces*
1 cup celery root, sliced and cut in bite-
*   size pieces*
1 cup fresh small wild mushrooms caps,
*   such as shiitake, cleaned with paper*
*   towels*

1 pound small zucchini, ends removed
*   and cut in ½-inch rounds*
Salt and freshly ground black pepper to
*   taste*

Heat the olive oil in a large Dutch oven on the stovetop, add the onion rings and paprika, reduce heat, cover and cook for 10 minutes. Add the pickle, turn up the heat, add the wine, and cook, uncovered, until the liquid is reduced to 1 tablespoon. Add the Vegetable Stock, cover, and simmer for 30 minutes.

Just before serving, place the carrots, potatoes, celery root, and mushroom caps in the stock, cover the pan, and simmer for 5 minutes. Add the zucchini and cook 2 minutes more. Season with the salt and pepper. With a slotted spoon, distribute the vegetables among 6 plates and moisten with some of the stock.

Vidalia Onions Stuffed with Zucchini

Vidalias are among those vegetables with a fairly short season. They are extremely sweet, as onions go, so they should not be substituted for the sharper onions that you use all the time.

Makes 6 servings

2 tablespoons butter, plus additional for
*   greasing baking dish and*
*   wax paper*
3 Vidalia onions, peeled
1 cup Chicken Stock (page 155) or
*   canned chicken broth*
1 pound small zucchini, cleaned
*   thoroughly, ends removed, and*
*   cut in julienne*
2 carrots, peeled and cut in julienne
2 tablespoons fresh thyme, stems removed
*   and minced*
Salt and freshly ground black pepper to
*   taste*
6 tablespoons grated Parmesan cheese
Thyme sprigs, for garnish

Preheat oven to 375°F. Butter a large baking dish. Cut a piece of wax paper large enough to cover the baking dish and brush one side with butter.

Bring about 3 quarts of salted water to a boil in a large pot. Place the onions in the water and simmer, covered, for 8 minutes. Gently remove them with a slotted spoon and, when cool enough to handle, cut them in half vertically. Remove the inner layers and reserve for another use, saving the two outer layers, together, for use as containers for the filling. Place about 12 "double layers," rounded side down, in the baking dish. Pour the stock on top.

Melt the 2 tablespoons of butter in large frying pan or wok, add the zucchini, carrots, minced thyme, salt, and pepper, and stir-fry for 3 minutes. Remove from the heat and stir in half the Parmesan.

Fill the onion containers with the vegetable mixture, sprinkle the remaining Parmesan on top, and bake for 15 minutes. Serve garnished with thyme sprigs.

Zucchini with Black Quinoa Filling

Zucchini harvest time is almost a national joke. But you can have the last laugh if you prepare yourself with a variety of recipes to use up the bounty. Here's one of my favorites.

Makes 6 servings

⅓ cup black quinoa
6 small zucchini, washed thoroughly, ends removed, halved lengthwise
Salt and freshly ground black pepper to taste
1 pound tomatoes
4 tablespoons (½ stick) butter plus additional to prepare baking dish and foil
1 large shallot, minced
1 bunch flat-leaf (Italian) parsley, tough stems removed, leaves rinsed, dried, and minced
1 sprig oregano, minced

Rinse the quinoa and soak in cold water for 30 minutes.

With the tip of a spoon or a melon-ball cutter, hollow out the zucchini, leaving a ¼-inch shell all around. Sprinkle lightly with salt, and place with hollow side down on paper towels to drain. Chop zucchini pulp, and set aside.

Bring about 1 cup of salted water to a boil in a 1-quart saucepan, drain quinoa, and stir into water. Reduce to a simmer, cover pan, and cook for 15 minutes. Drain, and spread on a baking sheet. Place the tomatoes in the boiling water for about 1 minute. Remove and when cooled, pull off skin, cut in half horizontally, and remove seeds. Chop and add to zucchini pulp.

Preheat the oven to 375°F, butter a large baking dish, and brush one side of a piece of aluminum foil with butter.

Melt the 4 tablespoons of butter over low heat, and cook the minced shallot until it is translucent. Stir in the zucchini pulp, tomato pieces, parsley, and oregano, and simmer, stirring occasionally, for 10 minutes. Add quinoa and blend well. Taste and adjust salt and pepper. Fill the zucchini shells with the mixture, packing it down firmly. Place in the baking dish, cover with the aluminum foil, and bake for 10 minutes.

Desserts

Want to see your friends' eyes light up? The word "dessert" is probably all you need to say. No matter where the meal is eaten, dessert is the last thing people eat, so it's the first thing that comes to mind. I remember a dinner party where a storebought cake was the last part of a lovingly prepared meal. It was pretty heavy and not very good, but everybody raved about it, simply because it was the last thing they remembered.

I would much rather improvise with the appetizer than rely on a storebought concoction for the all-important final impression of a meal. Also, I have some of my own rules for desserts, and I think they work pretty well. I want desserts that are light on the stomach, so I steer clear of heavy cakes. I also have a trick for cutting down on the amount of sugar I add—relying more on the natural sugars in dried fruits, such as apricots, currants, dates, and prunes.

Most of the recipes in this chapter use fresh berries or fruit, and, if possible, I use them raw, or else I simply poach or bake them.

All of these desserts can be prepared ahead of time.

Almond-Lime Tart with Mango and Blueberries

The idea for this dessert came to me when I was serving fresh berries with cookies. I thought that there was a better way to highlight both—and there was. So I turned the cookie into a tart and I made the fruit into a key player instead of an afterthought.

Makes 6 servings

Pastry:
1 cup flour
¼ cup finely ground almonds
¼ cup dark brown sugar
Pinch of salt
6 tablespoons unsalted butter, chilled and cut in pieces, plus some to prepare springform pan and foil

Filling:
⅓ cup sugar
2 extra-large eggs
½ teaspoon grated lime zest
¼ cup freshly squeezed lime juice
½ teaspoon baking powder
1 teaspoon cornstarch

Garnish:
1 mango
1 cup blueberries, rinsed and patted dry

Preheat oven to 350°F.

Blend the flour, almonds, brown sugar, and salt in a food processor. With the machine running, add the butter, a piece at a time, to make a dough. Using additional butter, grease a 13-inch springform pan, line the pan with aluminum foil, and grease the foil with butter. Press the dough into the pan and bake for 30 minutes.

Meanwhile, whisk together the sugar, eggs, lime zest, lime juice, baking powder, and cornstarch. Pour the mixture onto the hot crust, and bake for 15 minutes or until the filling is firm. Remove from the oven, release the lock of the springform pan, and let cool completely. Remove the side of the pan. Using a wide spatula, remove the bottom part of the springform pan, remove the foil from the pastry, and place the pastry on a serving plate. Cover with plastic wrap and refrigerate.

Peel the mango and cut it into thin slices. (The mango is slippery, so hold it with paper towels.) Refrigerate. Just before serving, place the mango slices, slightly overlapping each other, along the pastry rim. Place the blueberries in the center.

Apples with Black Currants and Rum Custard

Apples start out as a good health food, but dessert is dessert, after all. The simple rum custard can be replaced by vanilla ice cream.

Makes 6 servings

Poaching mixture:
1 cup dry white wine
1 tablespoon sugar
2 cloves
3 large tart apples, such as Winesaps or
*   Granny Smith*

Rum custard:
4 extra-large egg yolks
⅓ cup sugar
1 teaspoon cornstarch
2 tablespoons dark rum
¾ cup boiling milk
1 cup heavy cream

For serving:
6 macaroon cookies
6 tablespoons black currants in syrup

Combine the wine, 1 tablespoon of sugar, and cloves in a large saucepan and bring to a boil. Peel the apples, cut them in half horizontally, and remove the cores. Place the apples in the wine mixture, cover, and simmer for about 10 minutes.

Turn the apples and simmer for 10 minutes more. Test for doneness by sticking a knife tip into the thickest part of the apples. They should feel buttery. Remove the apples with a slotted spoon and let them cool. Discard the wine mixture.

Make the rum custard by blending the egg yolks, ⅓ cup of sugar, cornstarch, and rum in a mixing bowl. Set the bowl over a pan of boiling water and, using an electric beater at medium speed, whisk the custard for about 15 minutes or until it is pale yellow. Add the hot milk while stirring vigorously. Transfer the custard to a heavy-bottomed saucepan, and stir with a wooden spoon over low heat until thickened. Immediately remove from the heat, and stir until cooled. Refrigerate. Whip the heavy cream until firm peaks form and fold into the completely cooled custard.

Place the macaroons in a plastic bag, and crush them with a rolling pin.

Spread a few spoonfuls of custard into the centers of each of 6 dessert plates, and place an apple half, rounded side down, on the custard. Fill the apple cavities with macaroon crumbs. Sprinkle with the currants and drizzle the currant syrup on the custard.

Apricots with "Custard" on Puff Pastry

Good, fresh apricots are a glorious ingredient for dessert, but their short growing season can make them difficult to come by. When they're available, buy them. You'll be glad for recipes like this one, which is unusual if only because the custard has no eggs.

Makes 6 servings

1 sheet (9 x 9½ inches) frozen puff pastry
1 tablespoon sugar
12 large apricots, cut in half, pits removed
1 vanilla bean, halved lengthwise, seeds
*   scraped out and reserved*
½ cup water
¼ cup sugar

Custard:
1 cup whole milk
3 tablespoons sugar
1 tablespoon cornstarch
2 tablespoons Kirsch
1 cup heavy cream

Preheat oven to 375°F.

Partially defrost the pastry sheet for about 10 minutes. Unfold, and cut along the perforated lines and across the middle to make 6 even pieces. Pierce with a fork at 1-inch intervals and sprinkle the pastry surface with the 1 tablespoon of sugar. Place sugared surface up on a baking sheet and bake for 15 minutes or until lightly brown. Remove to a rack to cool.

Place the apricots, vanilla bean, seeds, water, and ¼ cup of sugar in a large saucepan, and simmer, covered, for 10 minutes. Remove the apricots with a slotted spoon and let them cool on a plate. Remove the vanilla bean, and boil the liquid until it has reduced to the consistency of syrup. Keep warm.

To make the custard, bring the milk, 3 tablespoons of sugar, and cornstarch to a boil, and stir vigorously over low heat until thickened. Remove from the heat, stir in the Kirsch, and cool completely. Whip the heavy cream until firm peaks form and blend into the custard.

To serve, place a piece of the puff pastry on each of 6 dessert plates, spoon some custard onto each piece, place 4 apricot halves, rounded sides up, on each pastry, and drizzle some warm apricot syrup on top of each. Serve immediately.

Baked Apples with Applejack Sauce

Good quality apples are available year round, are a staple in most households, and lend themselves to wonderful desserts. An assertive apple is best paired with an assertive sauce, such as the one in this recipe.

Makes 6 servings

Butter to prepare the baking dish
3 tablespoons sugar
3 large tart apples, such as Winesaps or
     Granny Smiths
½ cup finely ground almonds
1 teaspoon ground cinnamon
1 teaspoon grated lemon zest
¼ cup water

Sauce:
1 cup frozen apple-juice concentrate
1 tablespoon powdered gelatin
1 tablespoon apple-flavored brandy
½ cup sour cream

Preheat oven to 375°F. Grease a 9 x 13-inch baking dish with butter. Sprinkle the bottom of the dish with 1 tablespoon of the sugar.

Peel the apples, cut each in half horizontally, and scoop out the cores. Place the apple halves in the buttered dish. Combine the ground almonds, cinnamon, lemon zest, and the remaining sugar, and stuff apple cavities with the mixture. Add the water to the baking dish and bake for 25 minutes.

Meanwhile, make the sauce. Warm the apple-juice concentrate in a small saucepan, whisk in the gelatin, and bring to a boil, stirring constantly. Remove the saucepan from the heat, and stir vigorously until the gelatin dissolves. Add the brandy and let cool to room temperature.

Just before serving, stir the sour cream and the juices from the baking dish into the sauce. (If the sauce has set, place the saucepan over low heat before stirring in the sour cream.) Place a large spoonful of sauce into the center of each of 6 dessert plates, and top with the apple halves. Spoon the remaining sauce over the apples, and serve at room temperature.

Cardamom Pears

Pears are a time-honored foundation for desserts, and this one stresses flavor. The long baking time concentrates the flavor of the cardamom.

Makes 6 servings

1 cup frozen orange-juice concentrate
½ cup water
1 teaspoon orange extract
3 large, firm Bosc pears
1 teaspoon ground cardamom
1 cup homemade crème fraîche (page
*   157) or 6 ounces vanilla ice cream*

Preheat oven to 375°F. Blend the orange-juice concentrate, water, and orange extract. Set aside.

Peel the pears, and cut through the stems so you end up with two halves, each with a piece of stem. Remove the core with a melon-ball cutter, and cut each pear half into about 10 slices, leaving the top of the pear uncut. Arrange the pears in a 9 x 13-inch baking dish and press with your fingers so the pears fan out. Pour the orange mixture on top, and sprinkle the pears with the cardamom. Bake for 30 minutes.

Place a dollop of *crème fraîche* in the center of each of 6 dessert plates, top with a pear half, and spoon some warm orange sauce over the top. (If the sauce has hardened, add 1 tablespoon of water, stir and reheat.) Serve at room temperature.

Chocolate Mousse Cake
with Kirsch Cream and Raspberries

This chocolate cake is moist yet dense because it contains very little flour. Cut down on preparation time by replacing the Kirsch cream with whipped cream to which vanilla or orange extract has been added.

Makes 6 servings

Cake:
3 ounces good quality bittersweet chocolate
2 tablespoons water
6 tablespoons unsalted butter, softened and cut in small pieces
3 extra-large eggs, separated
¾ cup sugar
Pinch of salt
¼ cup cake flour, sifted twice

Kirsch cream:
3 extra-large eggs
⅓ cup sugar
1 cup milk, heated
2 tablespoons Kirsch
Pinch of salt

For serving:
1 pint fresh raspberries

Place the chocolate with the 2 tablespoons of water in a small saucepan over low heat. As soon as chocolate starts to melt, add the butter a piece at a time, stirring constantly. As soon as chocolate has melted, remove the pan from the heat. In a medium bowl, beat the egg yolks and gradually stir in the ¾ cup of sugar until the mixture is pale yellow. Stir the chocolate into the egg mixture.

Add the pinch of salt to the egg whites, and beat until peaks form. Fold about a quarter of the egg whites into the chocolate mixture and blend in half of the flour. Add the remaining egg whites and the flour until you have a smooth batter.

Preheat oven to 375°F. Butter a 9-inch ring mold. Heat about 2 quarts water in kettle.

Pour the batter into the prepared ring mold and place the mold in a baking dish. Anchor it with a cast-iron lid or heavy pan, then pour hot water into the pan to come halfway up the ring mold. Place the pan in the oven and poach the cake for 40 minutes. Remove and let the cake cool in the ring mold for 30 minutes. Invert mold onto a plate, cover the cake loosely with plastic wrap, and refrigerate for at least 4 hours.

Make the cream by whisking the 3 egg yolks with the ⅓ cup of sugar in a bowl until the mixture is light yellow and creamy. Slowly add the hot milk, whisking constantly, and transfer to a heavy-bottomed saucepan. Set the saucepan over very low heat, whisking until the cream has thickened. Stir in the Kirsch and refrigerate until cooled. Whisk the 3 egg whites with the pinch of salt until stiff, fold into the cream, and chill until serving time.

To serve individual portions, spread some cream into the center of each of 6 dessert plates and place 2 1-inch-thick slices of cake on top. Garnish with some raspberries. Or, place the cake on a serving plate, spoon the cream into the center of the cake, and top with the raspberries.

Dried Fruit in Puff Pastry with Vanilla Sauce

The dried fruits in these pastries perfume your kitchen as they bake. You can also serve them "solo" or, for a lighter version, substitute the vanilla sauce with a fruit sorbet.

Makes 6 servings

Vanilla Sauce:
4 extra-large egg yolks
½ cup granulated sugar
1¼ cups hot milk
1 teaspoon cornstarch
1 tablespoon vanilla extract

Filling:
3 ounces pitted dates
¼ cup dried currants
4 dried figs, stems removed
½ cup whole almonds
1 teaspoon grated lemon zest
2 tablespoons lemon juice

Pastry:
1 sheet (9 x 9½ inches) frozen puff pastry
1 tablespoon superfine sugar
Butter, to prepare baking sheet

To make the vanilla sauce, beat the egg yolks with the granulated sugar until the mixture is pale yellow, add the hot milk and cornstarch, pour the mixture into a heavy-bottomed medium saucepan, and set the pan over low heat. Stir continuously until the sauce begins to thicken, then remove from the heat and continue stirring until the sauce has cooled. Beat in the vanilla extract, and refrigerate.

Make the filling by chopping the dates, currants, figs, and almonds in a food processor and blending in the lemon zest and lemon juice. Set aside

Preheat oven to 375°F.

Partially defrost the pastry sheet for about 10 minutes, and cut along the perforated lines to make 3 strips. Cut each strip across into 4 pieces, each 2½ inches square. Sprinkle the squares with the sugar and roll them out to about 4 x 4 inches, pressing the superfine sugar into the dough in the process. Turn the squares over so that the sugar coating is on the bottom, then place 1½ tablespoons of the filling into the center of each square. Bring together the opposite corners of each square to make a pouch and pinch the corners firmly with a twisting motion. Repeat with remaining pastry and filling. Place 2 inches apart on a greased cookie sheet, and bake for 20 minutes or until golden brown.

Place 2 pastries on each plate and spoon the vanilla sauce on top.

Figs with Raspberry Sauce

Fresh figs are always a treat, and they are so sweet that you'll enjoy them more by playing that sweetness against a tart sauce. That's where the raspberries come in.

Makes 6 servings

1 package (12 ounces) frozen raspberries
¼ cup sugar
2 tablespoons lemon juice
6 large or 12 small fresh mission figs
1 tablespoon Kirsch
1 cup heavy cream
¼ teaspoon vanilla extract

Defrost the raspberries, mix in half the sugar and all of the lemon juice, and purée in a food processor. Strain, pushing down on the pulp to extract as much fruit as possible. Refrigerate.

Wipe the figs with paper towels, cut off the stems, peel away the thin outer layer of skin, and make 4 vertical incisions in each, cutting almost to the bottom. Spread out the segments, sprinkle with the Kirsch, and set aside for 1 hour.

Just before serving, whip the heavy cream until firm peaks form. Stir in the remaining sugar and the vanilla extract. To serve, spread a thin layer of the whipped cream on the bottoms of each of 6 dessert plates. Make a bulls-eye with the raspberry sauce, and, using a toothpick, drag the color outward through the cream. Place the figs in the center of each plate and serve immediately.

Grand Marnier Apricot Sabayon

Sometimes a fresh ingredient is the only way to go, but many recipes work fine with a frozen or dried equivalent. So rather than being tyrannized by the apricot's short season, reach for dried apricots and try this dessert.

Makes 6 servings

16 ounces dried apricots, soaked in 2 cups
    cold water for 4 hours
4 extra-large egg yolks
⅓ cup sugar
¼ cup Grand Marnier or orange-flavored
    liqueur
1 teaspoon cornstarch
1 cup heavy cream, whipped
Sweet Palmiers (page 160)

Bring the soaked apricots and water to a boil in a saucepan, reduce the heat, and simmer, covered, for 30 minutes.

Using a slotted spoon, transfer the apricots to the workbowl of a food processor and purée. Boil the apricot soaking liquid until it's reduced to a syrup, and add to the puréed apricots.

Whisk the egg yolks, sugar, and liqueur until the mixture is pale yellow, and stir in the cornstarch. Set the bowl on the rim of a smaller saucepan containing simmering water (an improvised double-boiler). Stir constantly, keeping the water at a simmer until the mixture has lightly thickened. Cool the mixture, and combine with the puréed apricots.

Whip the heavy cream, fold it into the apricot mixture, place in a serving bowl, cover, and refrigerate for at least 4 hours before serving. Serve accompanied by Sweet Palmiers.

Mango Mousse with Mint

Well-ripened mangoes are a must for this refreshing dessert. To ripen this exotic, tangy fruit, place on a window sill until ready. They should yield slightly to the touch and have a floral aroma at the stem.

Makes 6 servings

4 mangoes, 2 yielding slightly to the
    touch, 2 very soft
3 tablespoons lemon juice
2 extra-large egg whites
5 tablespoons sugar
¼ cup water
¾ cup heavy cream
6 amaretto biscotti (optional)
Mint leaves, for garnish

    Peel the 2 firm mangoes (they're slippery, so hold them with paper towels), and dice. Refrigerate, covered. Scrape any flesh remaining on the pit into a small bowl, and cut and scrape the flesh from the soft mangoes as well. Purée, in batches if necessary, in the food processor, dividing the lemon juice among the batches.

    Beat the egg whites until soft peaks form, sprinkle with 1 tablespoon of the sugar, and beat until firm peaks form. Boil the water with the remaining sugar, and stir until the sugar has dissolved. Add to the egg whites and blend well. Whip the heavy cream until firm peaks form.

    Blend the mango purée into the egg whites, mix in the whipped cream, cover the bowl, and refrigerate for at least 4 hours.

    If you are using them, place the amaretto biscotti in a bag, close tightly, and crush them with a rolling pin.

    Just before serving, spread the mango mousse in centers of 6 shallow soup bowls, and top each with some of the diced mango. Sprinkle with the amaretto crumbs, and garnish with the mint leaves.

Oranges with Black Olives and Goat Cheese

Nothing makes a more unusual finale to a meal than a dessert made with ingredients most commonly used for savory dishes. They're often the best ones.

Makes 6 servings

½ pound goat cheese, such as
*   Montrachet*
6 blood or navel oranges
1 tablespoon olive oil
1 tablespoon balsamic vinegar
½ teaspoon salt
Freshly ground black pepper to taste
18 dry-cured Turkish or Moroccan olives,
*   pitted*

Place the goat cheese in the freezer for about 1 hour, then cut into 18 portions and refrigerate.

Cut each orange into 3 slices. Squeeze the ends to make ¼ cup of juice and blend the juice with the olive oil, vinegar, and salt to make a dressing. Set aside. Remove the rind and the white pith from the orange slices, and refrigerate.

About 1 hour before serving, divide the orange slices on individual plates, and top them with the goat cheese. Drizzle the orange dressing on top, and sprinkle with black pepper. Serve garnished with the olives.

Peach Pastries with Fresh Fig Purée and Berries

This is another dessert based on fruit with a short growing season. Make it when you can, but be aware of the alternatives to fresh peaches—large plums, nectarines, or apples.

Makes 6 servings

6 tablespoons unsalted butter, melted,
*   plus some to prepare cookie sheet*
8 amaretto biscotti
1 16-ounce package phyllo dough
3 well-ripened freestone peaches, cut in
*   half, pits discarded*
2 tablespoons superfine sugar
12 fresh mission figs
¼ cup granulated sugar
¼ cup lemon juice
1 tablespoon Grand Marnier or orange-
*   flavored liqueur*
½ cup heavy cream, whipped
1 cup raspberries
1 cup blueberries

Lightly brush a cookie sheet with some of the melted butter. Place the amaretto biscotti in a plastic bag, close tightly, and crush them with a rolling pin. Set aside.

Preheat oven to 375°F.

Cut out a 7-inch-square stack of phyllo dough and cover with a damp towel. (Save the remaining dough in the package for another use.) Lightly brush 1 sheet of dough with some of the melted butter, starting at the edges and moving to the center of the sheet. Repeat 3 more times, creating 4 layers.

Sprinkle each stack with 1 teaspoon of the amaretto crumbs and place half a peach, round side up, in the center of the phyllo dough. Gather together the edges of the dough, and pinch the top to make a pouch. Place on the baking sheet. Repeat to make 5 more pastries. Brush the outsides of the pastries with some melted butter, and sprinkle the superfine sugar on top. (The pouches can be prepared 4 hours ahead and refrigerated.) Bake on the middle shelf of the oven for 30 minutes.

Peel the figs and purée them with the granulated sugar, lemon juice, and liqueur in a food processor. Transfer to a mixing bowl. Whip the cream and fold into the fig purée.

Divide the fig cream among 6 dessert plates. Top with a peach pastry, and garnish with raspberries and blueberries.

Pears with Port Wine Cream

Poached pears are the favored ingredient for many desserts, and with good reason—their own wonderful flavor can be augmented by the poaching liquid. Here, the concentrated liquid emphasizes some favorite spices.

Makes 6 servings

2 cups water
3 tablespoons sugar
2 tablespoons lemon juice
1 cup Port wine
1 bay leaf
2 cloves
8 whole allspice
2-inch piece cinnamon stick
3 large Bosc or Bartlett pears,
*   with stems*
1 cup heavy cream
1 teaspoon ground cinnamon

Place the water, sugar, lemon juice, wine, bay leaf, cloves, allspice, and cinnamon stick in a large saucepan, bring to a boil, and reduce to a simmer.

Peel the pears without removing the stems. Hold each pear down while you halve it, cutting through the stem. You should end up with two halves, each with a piece of stem. Core the pears, and place them immediately into the simmering liquid to prevent discoloration. Cook until they are soft. Check after 10 minutes, but the actual cooking time will depend on the ripeness of the pears. They should feel buttery when pierced with the tip of a knife. Transfer the pears with a slotted spoon from the poaching liquid to a bowl. Cover and refrigerate.

Strain the poaching liquid into a small saucepan. Reduce the liquid until it has the consistency of syrup and brush the pears with the syrup. Whip the heavy cream until firm peaks form and blend the remaining syrup into the whipped cream.

Spread some cream in the center of each of 6 dessert plates, and top each with a pear half, rounded side up. Garnish the pears by dusting them lightly with ground cinnamon.

Prunes with Cinnamon Sauce

Ice cream is the perfect accompaniment to this dessert, but be sure you use an assertive ice cream. This recipe calls for ginger ice cream, which is a good example.

Makes 6 servings

1 can (9 ounces) pitted prunes
¼ cup candied orange peel
1 navel orange
2 tablespoons unsalted butter
1 tablespoon sugar
1 teaspoon vanilla extract
1½ cups dry red wine
2-inch piece of cinnamon stick
2 whole cloves
2 lemon slices
1 pint ginger ice cream (available in
*   specialty stores)*

Soak the prunes in cold water for 10 minutes, transfer them to a plate and stuff each with a portion of the candied orange peel. Slice the orange and squeeze the juice from the orange ends over the prunes. Reserve the orange slices.

Melt the butter in a large saucepan, add the sugar and vanilla extract, and cook until the sugar turns light brown. Add the prunes in a single layer and pour in the wine. Cover the pan, cook over medium heat for 3 minutes, and let the prunes cool in the wine.

Remove the prunes from the wine with a slotted spoon. Add the cinnamon stick, cloves, lemon and orange slices to the liquid. Cook over high heat until the wine has been reduced to ½ cup and has the consistency of syrup. Strain into a clean saucepan.

Just before serving, reheat the syrup. Place a scoop of ice cream in the center of each of 6 dessert plates, and surround the ice cream with 3 or 4 prunes. Spoon the warm syrup on top and serve immediately.

Pumpkin Custard with Praline

This is a lighter version of the traditional pumpkin pie. What you get here are the spicy flavors and the silky consistency of the pumpkin with the crunchy praline on top.

Makes 6 servings

Butter, for preparing cookie sheet and
   ramekins
¼ cup slivered almonds
3 tablespoons sugar
1 tablespoon water
1 can (15 ounces) solid-pack pumpkin
¼ cup milk
½ cup heavy cream
¼ cup sugar
1 extra-large egg
2 extra-large egg yolks
1 tablespoon ground cinnamon
1 teaspoon ground ginger
1 pint lemon sorbet

Use the butter to grease a cookie sheet and 6 ramekins.

To make the praline, place the almonds in a single layer on the prepared cookie sheet. Cook the sugar with the water in a saucepan until sugar is lightly brown. Immediately pour the sugar over the almonds and, when hardened, remove with a spatula. Place in a plastic bag, close tightly, and crush the praline with a rolling pin. You should be left with coarse crumbs; divide the crumbs among the ramekins.

Preheat oven to 375°F. Heat about 1 quart of water.

Place the pumpkin in a large bowl, add the milk, cream, sugar, egg, and egg yolks, and whisk for 3 minutes at high speed with an electric mixer. Stir in the cinnamon and ginger. Transfer the pumpkin mix to a pitcher. Carefully pour the mixture into the ramekins, set them in an 11 x 13-inch baking dish, set them in the oven, and carefully pour the hot water into the baking dish to come halfway up the sides of the ramekins. Bake for 30 minutes or longer. Test with a fork. If the tines come out clean, the custard is set. Let cool for 5 minutes, invert each custard onto individual dessert plates, and place a scoop of lemon sorbet next to each custard.

Raspberry Terrine

The flavor of raspberries is incomparable. Besides being so delicious by itself, it pairs brilliantly with other dessert ingredients. Chocolate is one, and orange is another. This recipe has three sources of orange flavor. You and your guests will love the result.

Makes 6 servings

1 bag (12 ounces) frozen, unsweetened
  raspberries
2 tablespoons corn syrup
3 extra-large egg yolks
¼ cup sugar
2 tablespoons orange-juice concentrate
1 tablespoon Grand Marnier or orange-
  flavored liqueur
¼ cup orange juice
1 envelope powdered gelatin
¾ cup heavy cream
6 meringues (storebought)
½ cup black currants in syrup, drained
Additional black currants in syrup,
  drained, for garnish

Line an 8 x 4 x 2½-inch loaf pan with plastic wrap. Hold the wrap in place with a rubber band placed along the outside of the rim of the pan.

Defrost the raspberries, and purée in a food processor. Strain, using a spatula to push down on the solids and extract as much pulp as possible. Stir in the corn syrup. To make a cream, whisk the egg yolks with the sugar until they are pale yellow. Add the orange juice concentrate and the liqueur, set the bowl over simmering water, and stir until the cream is thickened. (If the sauce does not thicken, the water in the saucepan isn't hot enough). Let the cream cool, and fold the raspberry purée into the cream. Heat the orange juice in a small saucepan, stir in the gelatin, whisk until the gelatin is completely dissolved, and add to the raspberry cream. Mix thoroughly. Whip the heavy cream until firm peaks form, and fold it into the raspberry cream. Place in the freezer for 15 minutes.

Line the loaf pan with the meringues by slicing them in half horizontally and trimming them to fit the bottom and the sides of the loaf pan. Add half the raspberry cream and top with a layer of the drained black currants. Spoon the remaining raspberry cream over the black currants. Cover the loaf pan with plastic wrap and freeze for 6 hours or more.

One hour before serving, remove the terrine from the freezer and remove the plastic cover and the rubber band. Turn upside down onto a serving dish and remove plastic lining. (If the terrine sticks to the pan, place a hot towel over the pan and wait a few minutes). To serve, cut into 1-inch slices and serve garnished with additional black currants.

Simple Apple Tart

Sometimes, basic is best, and an apple tart will always please. But even with old standards, I look for a new twist. Here, the tart apricot jelly and the crunchy corn flake crumb layer provide a surprise flavor and texture.

Makes 6 servings

Pastry:
1¼ cups unbleached flour
2 tablespoons sugar
1 teaspoon baking powder
Pinch of salt
1 teaspoon grated lemon zest
¼ pound (1 stick) unsalted, chilled butter, cut in pieces, plus some to prepare the pan
Ice water, if needed

Filling:
2 large tart apples, such as Winesap
2 tablespoons apricot preserves
2 tablespoons corn-flake crumbs
1 extra-large egg
¼ cup heavy cream
3 tablespoons sugar
1 tablespoon Kirsch
1 teaspoon cornstarch
½ teaspoon ground cinnamon

Preheat oven to 425°F.

Place the flour into the workbowl of a food processor, add the sugar, baking powder, salt, and lemon zest, and pulse briefly. With the machine running, add the ½ pound of butter a piece at a time until the dough holds together. (You may need a few drops of ice water.) Place the dough on a floured surface and knead it briefly into a smooth ball. Wrap in plastic wrap, and let it rest in the refrigerator for at least 30 minutes.

To make the filling, peel, halve, and core the apples, and cut them into slices ¹⁄₁₆ inch thick. Butter a 9-inch springform pan. Remove the dough from the refrigerator 30 minutes before rolling it out. Dust a work surface liberally with flour and roll the dough into a 10-inch circle. Transfer the dough to the pan and shape it by pushing the dough into the edges of the pan and pressing up to form a ¼-inch-high edge. Prick the dough with a fork. Spread the apricot preserves over the bottom, sprinkle with the corn-flake crumbs, and arrange the apple slices in a circle, overlapping one another. Bake for 15 minutes.

Reduce the oven heat to 350°F.

Combine the egg, heavy cream, 2 tablespoons of the sugar, Kirsch, and cornstarch, and spoon the mixture into the center of the tart, being careful not to let the mixture run over the edge of the pastry. Return the tart to the oven and bake for 35 minutes more. Combine the remaining 1 tablespoon of sugar and the cinnamon, sprinkle over the tart, and bake 10 minutes more, until golden. Serve at room temperature.

Beef Stock

The essence of any good sauce is its base and a beef stock is easy to prepare. As an alternative, there are good meat reductions, called demi-glace, available in specialty stores or by mail order. Follow manufacturer's instruction for the proper ratio.

Makes 6 cups

5 to 6 pounds meaty beef bones (shins or ribs)
2 veal knuckles
2 medium onions, unpeeled and halved
8 cloves garlic, unpeeled and left whole
2 cups water
4 stalks celery, rinsed and halved
3 medium carrots, peeled, trimmed, and cut in half
2 small turnips, cleaned, trimmed, and cut in half
2 bay leaves
2 cloves
1 teaspoon dried thyme
1 teaspoon marjoram
1 teaspoon whole black peppercorns

Set an oven rack on the middle position and preheat oven to 500°F.

Place the beef bones and the veal knuckles in a single layer on the bottom part of a broiler pan and roast for 10 minutes or until the bones are dark brown. Turn the bones, add the onions and garlic, and roast 10 minutes more, or until the bones, onions, and garlic are dark brown. (You may have to do this in two batches).

Remove the bones, onions, and garlic from the broiler pan with metal tongs and place them in a large stockpot. Discard the fat from the broiler pan, add the water, and scrape up any dried-on juices from the bottom of the pan and add to the stockpot. Add the celery, carrots, turnips, bay leaves, and cloves. Cover the bones completely with water, add the thyme, marjoram, and peppercorns, and bring to the boil. Reduce heat and simmer, uncovered, for 3 hours.

Remove the bones with a slotted spoon. Discard the bones, and strain the stock through a fine-meshed sieve or a colander lined with cheesecloth. Boil the stock to reduce to about 6 cups. Refrigerate overnight. Remove congealed fat from the surface, bring the stock to a boil, then divide among 1- or 2-cup containers. Refrigerate for up to 2 days, or freeze for later use.

Butter Ball 'Grape Sculpture'

Here is a special way to present butter. The butter balls may be rolled in fresh minced herbs or cracked black peppercorns.

Makes about 24 large and 18 small balls

1 pound unsalted butter
Fresh grape leaves or other dark green
*   leaves*

Dip a melon-ball cutter with both large- and small-size scoops in hot water before starting each ball. Scoop out a ball of butter and place it in a bowl filled with salted ice water. Using a slotted spoon, remove the butter balls from the ice water, and arrange them, round sides up, on the grape leaves to make them look like a grape cluster. (See illustration.)

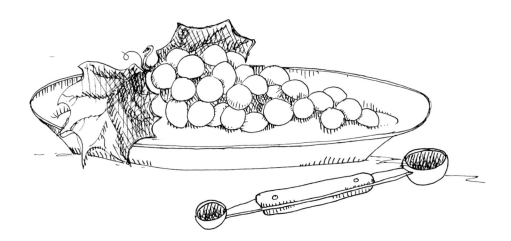

Cheese Board

Cheese can be served instead of a dessert. In addition to crusty bread, choose well-ripened pears or figs to go with your cheeses. Or serve them with crisp apples or grapes. Walnuts, pecans, and dried fruit are equally suitable. Select one cheese from each group for every six guests, and remove the cheese from the refrigerator two to four hours before serving. Here are some of my favorites:

Hard
Cabot "Private Stock" Cheddar
Comte or Gruyère
Gouda
Reggiano Parmesan or Provolone Auricchio

Semi-hard
Sonoma Jack
Port Salut or Morbier
Asiago fresca
Talegio
Roquefort

Soft
Cypress Grove or Crottin (Goat)
Explorateur or St. André
Delice du Gourmet or Tourree (Brie-type)
Mozzarella, plain or marinated in herbs
Maytag blue

Chicken Stock

I rarely bone my own chicken, but I always ask the poultry purveyor to package the bones separately. I freeze them until I have enough to make a stock. Canned broth can be used for soups, but they need to be reduced or their flavor bolstered by adding onions, celery, bay leaves, and cloves.

Makes 6 cups

6 pounds chicken bones plus 2 turkey
*   necks*
2 large, unpeeled onions, halved
2 bay leaves, fastened to the onions with 4
*   cloves*
4 cloves garlic, unpeeled and whole
4 stalks celery, cleaned and cut in half
3 medium carrots, peeled, trimmed, and
*   cut in half*
12 whole black peppercorns
1 cup water

Set an oven rack in the middle position, and preheat the oven to 500°F.

Spread half the bones in a single layer on the bottom part of a broiler pan, and roast them for 10 minutes or until brown. Turn the bones over, add 1 onion (and the bay leaf with the cloves) and 2 cloves of garlic, and continue roasting until the bones, onions, and garlic are brown, about 15 minutes.

Use tongs to remove the roasted bones, onions, and garlic, and place them in a stockpot with a capacity of at least 12 quarts. Repeat with the remaining bones, onion, and garlic, then add to the stockpot. Add the turkey necks, celery, carrots, and peppercorns, and cover the bones completely with water. Add the 1 cup of water to the broiler pan, scrape up any dried-on juices, and add them to the stockpot. Bring to the boil, reduce heat, and simmer, uncovered, for about 3 hours.

Remove the bones with a slotted spoon, and discard them. Strain the stock through a fine-meshed sieve into a large bowl. Rinse the stockpot, and return the stock to it. Boil to reduce to about 6 cups. Place in a medium saucepan, let cool, and refrigerate overnight. Remove and discard congealed fat from the stock, bring the stock to a boil, and divide into 1- or 2-cup containers. Refrigerate for up to 2 days, or freeze for later use.

Clarified Butter

Clarified butter can be used in all recipes that call for fresh butter. It allows sautéing at higher temperatures than fresh butter because the milky particles are what blacken first. Clarified butter can be stored in the refrigerator for several months.

Makes ⅔ cup

½ pound (2 sticks) unsalted butter

Cut each stick of butter in half, place the pieces in a glass measuring cup, and cover with plastic wrap (to prevent from splattering). Heat in microwave oven for 2 minutes on high and remove. Refrigerate for 2 hours, and, using a spoon, scrape off the white solids that have solidified on the top. The solidified yellow butterfat is the clarified butter. Discard the milky residue remaining in the measuring cup after the clarified butter has been used.

Crème Fraîche

I prefer *crème fraîche* to sour cream because of its delicate flavor and velvety consistency. It's simple to make; you just need to plan ahead. Use it in sauces and salad dressing or add sugar and it becomes a delicious accompaniment to fruit pies or fresh berries.

Makes about 1 cup

1 cup heavy cream
1 tablespoon buttermilk

In a large glass jar, whisk together the heavy cream and buttermilk. Cover the jar, shake, and store in a warm place, such as near the pilot of your stove, for 20 to 22 hours, or until it's lightly thickened and has the consistency of a soft pudding. If you'd like a thicker consistency, keep the mixture in a warm place for an additional 1 to 2 hours. Stir. Refrigerate for up to 2 weeks.

Fish Stock

Many stocks take a lot of time, but a flavorful fish stock can be prepared in less than an hour.

Makes 8 cups

6 pounds bones from non-oily fish, such
*   as red snapper, rockfish, whiting, or*
*   sea bass*
¼ cup olive oil
1 large leek, trimmed, thoroughly washed,
*   and chopped*
2 large stalks celery, rinsed and chopped
1 large onion, skin on, with 1 bay leaf
*   fastened with 2 cloves*
1 cup dry white wine
4 quarts water
6 whole black peppercorns
2 large sprigs parsley, rinsed
1 sprig fresh thyme
2 tablespoons lemon juice
Salt and freshly ground black pepper to
*   taste*

Rinse the fish bones, and cut them, if necessary, to fit into a large Dutch oven. Warm the olive oil in the Dutch oven, add the leeks, celery, whole onion, and fish bones, and cook on the stovetop, covered, over the lowest heat for 20 minutes. Add the wine, water, peppercorns, parsley, and thyme, and boil, uncovered, for 30 minutes. Remove and discard any impurities that form on the surface during the cooking.

Strain the stock through a fine-meshed sieve or a colander lined with cheesecloth into a fresh pan. Boil and reduce liquid to 2 quarts. Stir in the lemon juice, salt, and pepper. Divide among 2-cup containers. Refrigerate for up to 2 days or freeze for later use.

Mushroom Stock

The characteristic flavor of the wild mushrooms in this stock adds interest to soups and to vegetable and rice dishes. If reduced fat is on your agenda, try this for poaching chicken or fish.

Makes 6 cups

1 cup dried porcini mushrooms, rinsed and soaked in 2 cups water for 2 hours
1 onion, coarsely chopped
¼ cup Madeira wine
2 quarts water
2 pounds white mushrooms, cleaned with a damp paper towel and sliced
1 tablespoon lemon juice
1 tablespoon salt
1 teaspoon pepper

Drain the porcini mushrooms and reserve the soaking liquid. Cook the onion, covered, on the stovetop in a Dutch oven over very low heat. When the onions are softened, add the Madeira and turn up the heat. Cook, uncovered, until the wine is reduced to 2 tablespoons.

Add the water and both mushrooms. Strain the soaking liquid from the porcini mushroom through a fine-meshed sieve, add to the stock, and simmer, covered, for 2 hours. Line a colander with cheesecloth, strain the stock, transfer the stock to a clean saucepan, and boil over high heat until the liquid is reduced to 6 cups. Add the lemon juice, salt, and pepper.

Divide the stock among 2-cup containers, and refrigerate for up to 2 days or freeze for later use.

Palmiers

These pastries are easy to make by using frozen puff-pastry dough, and you can make both sweet and savory versions. Serve the sweet version with ice cream or fruits. The cheese-coated savory version, flavorful and pretty, can be used as a substitute for bread. Puff pastry is available in the frozen-foods section of most supermarkets.

1 sheet frozen puff pastry (9 x 9½ inches)
¼ cup superfine sugar (if you're making the sweet version)
½ cup finely grated Gruyère cheese (if you're making the savory version)

Defrost the puff pastry for 30 minutes, unfold, and cut along the perforation to make 3 strips.

If you're making the sweet version, spread half the sugar on your work surface, place the strips on top, and sprinkle the remaining sugar evenly over the surface. With a rolling pin, press the sugar into the pastry and, at the same time, roll out the dough to make 3 strips, each 16 inches long.

If you're making the savory version, use the cheese instead of the sugar.

Place each strip with the long dimension in front of you, fold in 2 inches from each side, and fold each side over twice more in the same manner to meet in the center. You will have 4 layers on each side. Fold the two parts together, making 8 layers. Press the two parts lightly together with a rolling pin and refrigerate for 30 minutes.

Preheat oven to 350°F.

With a serrated knife, cut the pastry crosswise into ½-inch-wide slices. Place the slices cut side down and 3 inches apart on a nonstick baking sheet. Bake for 10 minutes, or until golden. Turn and bake 10 more minutes.

Roasted Peppers

Many commercial versions of roasted peppers are of very good quality, but it's also an easy recipe to do at home, yielding an ingredient for many recipes.

6 red bell peppers, about 2½ pounds

Preheat the broiler. Place the peppers on a baking pan on the top shelf of the oven, and broil until the skins are charred, about 3 minutes. Turn the peppers until their skins are blistered evenly all around. Let the peppers cool, peel off the skins, cut them in half, and pull out the stem sections with the seeds attached to it.

Salads and Dressings

Putting together a well-balanced salad has become extremely simple. Mixed salad greens (also sold as mesclun), a combination of several baby greens of distinctive flavors and textures, are now available in most grocery stores. Or vary the greens according to season. The delicate greens need very little dressing so as not to overwhelm their subtle flavors. A quick way to toss and serve a salad is to line up 6 salad plates, and, with your hands covered with plastic bags, to toss and arrange the greens.

Makes 6 servings

Traditional

1 tablespoon balsamic vinegar
Pinch of curry powder
1 teaspoon Dijon mustard
1 teaspoon lemon juice
⅛ teaspoon salt or to taste
10 cups mixed salad greens, rinsed and
*   thoroughly dried and chilled*
¼ cup extra-virgin olive oil

Blend the vinegar, curry powder, mustard, lemon juice, and salt in a small bowl. When ready to serve, place the salad in a large mixing bowl, toss it with the olive oil, add the vinegar mixture, and toss again.

Piquant

1 tablespoon wasabi powder
1 tablespoon water

2 tablespoons rice wine vinegar
1 teaspoon soy sauce
⅓ cup safflower oil
10 cups mixed salad greens, rinsed and
*   thoroughly dried and chilled*
1 bunch scallions, trimmed, rinsed, and
*   minced*
2 tablespoons sesame oil

Combine the wasabi powder and water and let sit for 2 minutes to form a paste. Form the wasabi paste into a ball and set aside. Blend the vinegar, soy sauce, and safflower oil in a large bowl and whisk in the wasabi. When ready to serve, add the salad greens, scallions, and sesame oil, and toss.

Citrus

2 large tomatillos, papery husks removed,
*   soaked in boiling water for 30*
*   seconds to remove bitterness*
1 small clove garlic, minced
2 tablespoons lime juice
¼ teaspoon grated lime zest
2 tablespoons soy sauce
Pinch of sugar
Freshly ground black pepper to taste
¼ cup walnut oil
10 cups mixed salad greens, rinsed and
*   thoroughly dried and chilled*

Purée the tomatillos in a food processor. Place the purée in a small bowl and add the garlic, lime juice, zest, soy sauce, sugar, and pepper. When ready to serve, place the salad greens in a large mixing bowl, drizzle the walnut oil on top, and toss. Add the tomatillo purée, and toss again.

Three-in-One Tomato Sauce

If you are a novice, tomato sauce is a wonderful dish to begin with. Prepare all three of them, invite your friends, and let your guests help themselves to their favored sauce. One pound of pasta serves 3 people.

Makes 6 cups

2 stalks celery, rinsed and cut into 6 pieces
2 carrots, peeled and cut into 6 pieces
1 leek, outer leaves removed, roots trimmed, halved lengthwise, and cleaned thoroughly
4 cloves garlic
¼ cup olive oil
1 medium onion, peeled
2 cans (28 ounces each) crushed tomatoes
Salt and freshly ground black pepper to taste

To make the basic tomato sauce, mince the celery, carrot, leek, garlic, and onion in the workbowl of a food processor. Heat the olive oil in a Dutch oven on the stovetop, and cook the minced mixture over the lowest possible heat for 20 minutes. Add the tomatoes and simmer the sauce for 20 minutes. Add salt and freshly ground pepper to taste and you now have a basic tomato sauce. *Or,* make 3 distinct tomato sauces by dividing the basic tomato sauce into 3 saucepans and giving it added flavor by using the following ingredients:

Italian

1 sprig each fresh thyme, basil, and oregano, tied together
3 tablespoons hot pepper, minced

Add the herbs to the sauce, and simmer for 30 minutes. Remove the herb bundle before serving.

Mexican

2 tablespoons chili powder
1 tablespoon ground cumin

Add the chili powder and cumin to the sauce and simmer for 15 minutes.

Indian

2 tablespoons garam masala (available in Asian markets)
¼ teaspoon ground cloves

Add the *garam masala* and cloves to the sauce and simmer for 15 minutes.

Vegetable Stock

This fragrant vegetable stock lends itself well to soups or rice dishes or to poaching chicken. However, it lacks body so therefore is not suitable for sauces.

Makes 6 cups

2 cups carrots, peeled and coarsely chopped
2 large leeks, trimmed, rinsed thoroughly, and chopped
2 large stalks celery, coarsely chopped
1 small celery root with skin, scrubbed and quartered
2 large onions, skin on, studded with 1 bay leaf attached with 2 cloves
1 head garlic, halved with skin on
3 tablespoons olive oil
1 tablespoon dried thyme
1 tablespoon whole black peppercorns
2 cups water
2 tablespoons tomato purée
2 tablespoons miso paste

Set a rack on the middle position in the oven, and preheat oven to 450°F.

Toss the carrots, leeks, celery, celery root, onions, and garlic with the olive oil, and place in a broiler pan. Roast in the oven, tossing occasionally until brown, about 15 minutes. Transfer to a large stockpot, and add the thyme and peppercorns. Add the water to the roasting pan, scrape up any dried-on vegetable juices, place in the stockpot, and add enough water to cover the vegetables completely.

Bring the mixture to a boil, add the tomato purée and miso paste, reduce heat to a simmer, and cook, uncovered, for 1 hour.

Remove and discard the vegetables and strain the stock through a fine-meshed sieve or a sieve lined with cheesecloth. Return the strained liquid to a clean stockpot, and boil, uncovered, to reduce to 6 cups. Divide among 2-cup containers, and refrigerate up to 2 days or freeze for later use.

Glossary

Bake. A cooking method especially suitable for poultry that has been browned briefly on both sides. It can be further baked, without adding any fat, by covering it with foil in a hot oven. Check the oven temperature for accuracy and meticulously follow the oven temperature given in the recipe.

Blanch. Blanching almost always refers to a method of cooking vegetables. The vegetables are placed in boiling, salted water for a short time, and, when removed, placed in ice-cold water to abruptly halt the cooking process and to preserve the color. Tomatoes and peaches are blanched briefly to help remove their skins. Blanching cabbage leaves makes them pliable for use as a wrapping and also removes their strong flavor.

Boil. Boiling is used mostly for cooking pasta, rice, and dried beans. Boiling liquid has bubbles all over its surface. The pan is almost never covered.

Crème Fraîche. *Crème fraîche* is fermented cream that is much lighter than sour cream. It used to be that *crème fraîche* was almost always homemade because it was so difficult to buy. Although it's pretty easily made at home, it is now widely available, particularly at specialty food stores.

Cube. Often used to describe a vegetable that is cut in 1-inch cubes before it is used in a recipe.

Demi-glace. A demi-glace takes stock to the next step of intensity. When a cook makes a demi-glace, it means that the stock is reduced by half its volume. The result is a very intensely flavored liquid.

Dice. Dicing a food, often a vegetable, means cutting it in tiny cubes before using it in a recipe.

Fold. When one ingredient, usually egg whites or whipped cream, is folded into a batter, the two are combined delicately so as to preserve their air pockets.

Julienne. This word, often used as a noun or a verb, refers to a vegetable cut that makes the vegetable look like a pile of matchsticks. The usual dimension of each piece is $\frac{1}{16}$ of an inch thick and 2 inches long.

Mince. A minced ingredient is chopped very finely. It often refers to herbs, garlic, or citrus zests.

Mousse. A mousse is a purée of vegetable, meat, or fish that's lightened with the addition of whipped cream or egg whites.

Poach. A poached ingredient is cooked fully submerged in liquid that's barely moving. If the liquid is producing bubbles all over the pan, it is boiling. Poached foods retain their flavor and texture.

Purée. This is another cooking term commonly used as either a noun or a verb. A puréed food has been cooked and then mashed, usually in a food processor or blender, to a paste-like consistency, often in combination with herbs and flavorful soft or liquid ingredients.

Reduce. Reducing is an important step in making sauces. Stock or wine is cooked over high heat until it reaches the desired consistency. The liquid generally thickens and becomes more intensely flavored as it reduces.

Sauté. Sautéing is a cooking method used for meat, fish, and sometimes vegetables. It means to brown thoroughly dried food in a hot frying pan or skillet. It's often done in batches with meat that may be dusted with flour.

Simmer. When food is cooked in simmering water or stock, the liquid has only the slightest movement on the surface. In many cases, the liquid is brought to a boil, then reduced to a simmer while the food finishes cooking.

Zest. The outer, colored layer of a citrus fruit, usually either grated or cut into julienne strips. The zest is usually removed from the fruit with either a vegetable peeler or a grater, depending on how it will be used in a recipe. Zest should always be free of the underlying white layer of pith, which is bitter.

Index

Acorn Squash with Bulgur Wheat Filling, 84

Almond-Lime Tart with Mango and Blueberries, 133

Almond Parsley Dressing, Pasta with, 98

Anchovy Pesto, Turkey Tenderloin with, 38

Anchovy Toast, Yellow Tomato Soup with, 61

Appaloosa Beans with Avocado Topping, 85

Appetizer, 63–80

    Artichokes, Baby, with Carrots and Champagne Vinegar, 64

    Avocado with Shrimp, 63

    Cucumber Wheels with Crabmeat and Sushi Rice, 65

    Fennel with Smoked Salmon, 66

    Fettuccine with Smoked Salmon and Escarole Sauce, 67

    Goat Cheese Napoleons, 69

    Salmon Fillets with Salmon Roe, 70

    Salmon Fillets Wrapped in Seaweed, 71

    Sea Scallops and Green Beans with Watercress Sauce, 72

    Sea Scallops, in Phyllo with Red Cabbage, 73

    Shrimp Toast with Cognac Sauce, 74

    Shrimp Wrapped in Cabbage with Maple Syrup Sauce, 75

    Snow Peas and Endive with Shiitake Mushrooms, 76

    Spinach-Bluefish Ravioli, 77

    Two-Tiered Salad with Smoked Salmon and Goat Cheese, 78

    Vegetable-Salmon Terrine with Tomato Dill Sauce, 79

Apple(s)

    Baked, with Applejack Sauce, 136

    with Black Currants and Rum Custard, 134

    Tart, Simple, 149

Apricot Sabayon, Grand Marnier, 141

Apricots with "Custard" on Puff Pastry, 135

Artichoke(s)

    Baby, with Carrots and Champagne Vinegar, 64

    Bottoms with Shiitake Mushrooms, 112

    Green Peppercorns and Pastry Hearts, Chicken Breasts with, 7

    Soup with Mint, 49

Avocado with Shrimp, 63

Avocado Topping, Appaloosa Beans with, 85

Bacon and Pine Nuts, Collard Green Rolls with, 120

Bacon and Vinegar, Red Lentils with, 101

Baked Apples with Applejack Sauce, 136

Barley Risotto with Basil and Tomatoes, 86

Barley Soup with Oysters, 50

Basmati Rice

    with Cardamom Seeds and Garam Masala, 87

    Crabmeat Risotto, 92

    Curried Rice with Red Lentils, 93

Bean(s)

    Appaloosa, with Avocado Topping, 85

    Black, with Tomatillos, 88

    Salad, Three-, with Sun-Dried Tomatoes, 106

Beef Stock, 152

Belgian Endive with Green Beans and Poppy Seeds, 113

(Belgian) Endive and Snow Peas with Shiitake Mushrooms, 76

Black Beans with Tomatillos, 88

Blueberries and Mango, Almond-Lime Tart with, 133

Broccoli and Cauliflower with Ginger Sauce, 119

Brussels Sprouts with Peanuts, 114

Bulgur Vegetable Pilaf, 89

Bulgur Wheat Filling, Acorn Squash with, 84

Butter Ball "Grape Sculpture," 153

Butter, Clarified, 156

Cabbage

    Red, Sea Scallops in Phyllo with, 73

    Rolls with Vegetables, 115

    Shrimp Wrapped in, with Maple Syrup Sauce, 75

Cake, Chocolate Mousse, with Kirsch Cream and Raspberries, 138

Cardamom Pears, 137

Carrots

    with Basil Hollandaise, 117

    and Champagne Vinegar, Baby Artichokes with, 64

    with Marsala Wine, 118

    and Turnips with Parsley and Orange, 116

Cauliflower and Broccoli with Ginger Sauce, 119

Celery Root Soup with Caviar Toast, 51

Cheese Board, 154. *See also* Goat Cheese

Chicken, 3–29. *See also* Chicken Breasts; Chicken
   Thighs; Duck; Turkey
     about parts of, 2
     Grilled, with Kumquats, 34
     Grilled, with Tomatillos, 35
     Stock, 155
     Whole Boiled, 6
Chicken Breasts
     with Artichokes, Green Peppercorns and
       Pastry Hearts, 7
     with Black Currants and Pink Peppercorns, 8
     with Capers and Pimientos, 9
     Cold, with Cantaloupe and Fresh Mint, 25
     Cold, with Honey and Star Anise, 26
     Cold, with Lemon and Caper Dressing, 27
     Cold, with Oranges and a Green Dressing, 28
     Cold, with Szechuan Peppercorns and
       Pancakes, 29
     with Cornmeal Rounds and Tomato Sauce, 10
     with Curry Sauce, Dates, and Grapefruit, 11
     Filled with Goat Cheese and Nasturtium, 13
     Fingers with Cucumber and Dill, 19
     Fingers with Lingonberry Sauce, 20
     with Ginger and Lime, 12
     Grilled, 3
     with Juniper Berries, 14
     with Mango Chutney and Green Beans, 15
     with Peanut Crust and Port Wine, 16
     Poached, 4
     Sautéed, 5
     with Vegetables and Champagne Sauce, 18
     Wrapped in Poblano Chiles, 17
Chicken Thighs
     with Fragrant Vegetables, 21
     with Red Wine Sauce, 22
     with Two Paprikas, 23
     with Yellow Lentils and Cilantro, 24
Chocolate Mousse Cake with Kirsch Cream and
   Raspberries, 138
Chowder, Vegetable, en Croûte, 60
Clarified Butter, 156
Cod, Snow Pea Soup with, 58
Collard Green Rolls with Bacon and Pine Nuts, 120
Corn Grits Soufflé, White, 109
Cornmeal. *See also* Polenta
     Gratin with Fontina Cheese and Tomatoes, 90
     Hearts with Maple Glazed Onions, 91
     Rounds and Tomato Sauce, Chicken Breasts
       with, 10
Crabmeat Risotto, 92
Crabmeat and Sushi Rice, Cucumber Wheels with,
   65

Crème Fraîche, 157
Cucumber
     and Fresh Tarragon, Spaghetti with, 103
     -Rice Soup with Mint, 52
     Wheels with Crabmeat and Sushi Rice, 65
Currants, Black, and Rum Custard, Apples with,
   134
Curried Mussel Soup with Leek, 53
Curried Rice with Red Lentils, 93

Dessert, 133–149. *See also* Cheese Board
     Almond-Lime Tart with Mango and
       Blueberries, 133
     Apple Tart, Simple, 149
     Apples, Baked with Applejack Sauce, 136
     Apples with Black Currants and Rum
       Custard, 134
     Apricots with "Custard" on Puff Pastry, 135
     Cardamom Pears, 137
     Chocolate Mousse Cake with Kirsch Cream
       and Raspberries, 138
     Dried Fruit in Puff Pastry with Vanilla Sauce,
       139
     Figs with Raspberry Sauce, 140
     Grand Marnier Apricot Sabayon, 141
     Mango Mousse with Mint, 142
     Oranges with Black Olives and Goat Cheese,
       143
     Peach Pastries with Fresh Fig Purée and
       Berries, 144
     Pears with Port Wine Cream, 145
     Prunes with Cinnamon Sauce, 146
     Pumpkin Custard with Praline, 147
     Raspberry Terrine, 148
Dressing. *See* Salad Dressing
Dried Fruit in Puff Pastry with Vanilla Sauce, 139
Duck Breasts, 32
Duck Breasts with Apples and Cider Sauce, 33
Dumplings, Mini-, with Poppy Seeds, 96

Endive, Belgian, with Green Beans and Poppy
   Seeds, 113
Endive (Belgian) and Snow Peas, with Shiitake
   Mushrooms, 76
Escarole Soup with Smoked Salmon, 54

Fennel
     with Fennel Seeds and Lemon, 121
     with Smoked Salmon, 66
     Soup with Shrimp, 55
Fettuccine with Smoked Salmon and Escarole
   Sauce, 67

Figs, Fresh, Turkey Tenderloin with, and Port Wine Sauce, 41
Figs with Raspberry Sauce, 140
Fish. *See also* Shellfish
    Bluefish-Spinach Ravioli, 77
    Cod, Snow Pea Soup with, 58
    Monkfish, Sweet Pea Soup with, 59
    Salmon Fillets with Salmon Roe, 70
    Salmon Fillets Wrapped in Seaweed, 71
    Salmon-Vegetable Terrine with Tomato Dill Sauce, 79
    Stock, 158
Flour Pancakes, 30
Fruit, Dried, in Puff Pastry with Vanilla Sauce, 139

Gazpacho, Red Pepper, with Hummus Toast, 56
Glossary, 166–167
Goat Cheese
    Napoleons, 69
    and Nasturtium, Chicken Breasts Filled with, 13
    Oranges with Black Olives and, 143
    and Smoked Salmon, Two-Tiered Salad with, 78
    and Yellow Tomato Sauce, Leek Pastries with, 125
Grains. *See* Barley; Beans; Bulgur; Cornmeal; Grits; Lentils; Pasta; Rice
Grand Marnier Apricot Sabayon, 141
Green Beans
    Belgian Endive with, and Poppy Seeds, 113
    and Sea Scallops with Watercress Sauce, 72
    with Sunflower Seeds and Walnut Oil, 122
Grilled Chicken with Kumquats, 34
Grilled Chicken with Tomatillos, 35
Grits, White Corn, Soufflé, 109

Hearts of Palm with Zucchini and Red Peppers, 123

Individual Spinach Lasagna, 94

Kale with Olive Oil and Garlic, 124
Kashi with Crisp Prosciutto and Sage, 95

Lasagna, Spinach, Individual, 94
Leek Pastries with Goat Cheese and Yellow Tomato Sauce, 125
Lentils
    Red, with Bacon and Vinegar, 101
    Red, Curried Rice with, 93
    Yellow, Chicken Thighs with, and Cilantro, 24

Mango and Blueberries, Almond-Lime Tart with, 133
Mango Mousse with Mint, 142
Microwave, about using, 2
Mini-Dumplings with Poppy Seeds, 96
Monkfish, Sweet Pea Soup with, 59
Mousse, Chocolate, Cake with Kirsch Cream and Raspberries, 138
Mousse, Mango, with Mint, 142
Mushroom(s)
    Roasted, Soup with Scallion Toast, 57
    Shiitake, Artichoke Bottoms with, 112
    Shiitake, Snow Peas and Endive with, 76
    Stock, 159
Mussel Soup, Curried, with Leek, 53

Onions, Maple Glazed, Cornmeal Hearts with, 91
Onions, Vidalia, Stuffed with Zucchini, 129
Orange-Flavored Rice, 97
Oranges with Black Olives and Goat Cheese, 143
Oysters, Barley Soup with, 50

Palmiers (pastries), 160
Pancakes, Flour, 30
Pasta
    with Almond Parsley Dressing, 98
    Fettuccine with Smoked Salmon and Escarole Sauce, 67
    Lasagna, Spinach, Individual, 94
    Ravioli, Spinach-Bluefish, 77
    with Scallion Dressing, 99
    Spaghetti with Cucumber and Fresh Tarragon, 103
    Spinach, with Salmon Butter, 105
Pea. *See* Snow Pea; Sweet Pea
Peach Pastries with Fresh Fig Purée and Berries, 144
Pears, Cardamom, 137
Pears with Port Wine Cream, 145
Peppers, Roasted, 161. *See also* Red Peppers
Pesto, Almond Parsley Dressing, 98
Pesto, Anchovy, Turkey Tenderloin with, 38
Pilaf, Bulgur Vegetable, 89
Pilaf, Rice, Spicy, 104
Pistachio Filling, Potatoes with, 100
Polenta, Vegetable, 108
Potatoes, with Pistachio Filling, 100
poultry, about parts of, 2
Prosciutto, Crisp, and Sage, Kashi with, 95
Prunes with Cinnamon Sauce, 146
Puff Pastry, Apricots with "Custard" on, 135
Puff Pastry, Dried Fruit in, with Vanilla Sauce, 139

Pumpkin Custard with Praline, 147

Quinoa Filling, Zucchini Stuffed with, 130

Raspberry Sauce, Figs with, 140
Raspberry Terrine, 148
Ravioli, Spinach-Bluefish, 77
Red Pepper(s)
    Gazpacho with Hummus Toast, 56
    Roasted, 161
    and Zucchini, Hearts of Palm with, 123
Rice. *See also* Basmati Rice; Risotto
    -Cucumber Soup with Mint, 52
    Curried, with Red Lentils, 93
    Orange-Flavored, 97
    Pilaf, Spicy, 104
    Sushi, and Crabmeat, Cucumber Wheels with,
      65
    Two-Colored, 107
Risotto
    Barley, with Basil and Tomatoes, 86
    Crabmeat, 92
    Saffron, with Three Vegetables, 102
Roasted Peppers, 161

Saffron Risotto with Three Vegetables, 102
Salad. *See also* Chicken Breasts, Cold
    about, 162
    Three-Bean, with Sun-Dried Tomatoes, 106
    Two-Tiered, with Smoked Salmon and Goat
      Cheese, 78
Salad Dressing
    Citrus, 162
    Piquant, 162
    Traditional, 162
Salmon. *See also* Smoked Salmon
    Fillets with Salmon Roe, 70
    Fillets Wrapped in Seaweed, 71
    -Vegetable Terrine with Tomato Dill Sauce,
      79
Sauce, Tomato-Dill, 80
Sauce, Tomato, Three-in-One, 163
Scallion Dressing, Pasta with, 99
Scallion Toast, Roasted Mushroom Soup with, 57
Scallops, Sea, and Green Beans with with
    Watercress Sauce, 72
Scallops, Sea, in Phyllo with Red Cabbage, 73
Shellfish. *See* Crab; Mussel; Oysters; Scallops;
    Shrimp
Shiitake. *See* Mushrooms
Shrimp
    Avocado with, 63

Fennel Soup with, 55
Toast with Cognac Sauce, 74
Wrapped in Cabbage with Maple Syrup
    Sauce, 75
Smoked Bluefish-Spinach Ravioli, 77
Smoked Salmon
    and Escarole Sauce, Fettuccine with, 67
    Escarole Soup with, 54
    Fennel with, 66
    and Goat Cheese, Two-Tiered Salad with, 78
Smoked Turkey Breast with Grapes and
    Horseradish Dressing, 31
Snow Pea Soup with Cod, 58
Snow Peas and Endive with Shiitake Mushrooms,
    76
Soufflé, White Corn Grits, 109
Soup, 49–61. *See also* Stock
    Artichoke, with Mint, 49
    Barley, with Oysters, 50
    Celery Root, with Caviar Toast, 51
    Cucumber-Rice, with Mint, 52
    Curried Mussel, with Leek, 53
    Escarole, with Smoked Salmon, 54
    Fennel, with Shrimp, 55
    Gazpacho, Red Pepper, with Hummus Toast,
      56
    Roasted Mushroom, with Scallion Toast, 57
    Snow Pea, with Cod, 58
    Sweet Pea, with Monkfish, 59
    Vegetable Chowder en Croûte, 60
    Yellow Tomato, with Anchovy Toast, 61
Spaghetti with Cucumber and Fresh Tarragon, 103
Spinach
    -Bluefish Ravioli, 77
    Lasagna, Individual, 94
    Pasta with Salmon Butter, 105
Squash, Acorn, with Bulgur Wheat Filling, 84
Stock
    Beef, 152
    Chicken, 155
    Fish, 158
    Mushroom, 159
    Vegetable, 164
Sushi Rice and Crabmeat, Cucumber Wheels with,
    65
Sweet Pea Soup with Monkfish, 59
Swiss Chard Gratin, 126
Swiss Chard with Green Hollandaise, 127

Tart, Almond-Lime with Mango and Blueberries,
    133
Tart, Apple, Simple, 149

Tenderloin. *See* Turkey Tenderloin
Three-Bean Salad with Sun-Dried Tomatoes, 106
Three-in-One Tomato Sauce, 163
Tomatillos, Black Beans with, 88
Tomatillos, Grilled Chicken with, 35
Tomato(es)
    -Dill Sauce, 80
    Sauce, Three-in-One, 163
    Sun-Dried, Three-Bean Salad with, 106
    Yellow, Soup, with Anchovy Toast, 61
Turkey. *See also* Turkey Tenderloin
    about parts of, 2
    Breast with Gewürztraminer and Green
      Relish, 45
    Breast, Smoked, with Grapes and Horseradish
      Dressing, 31
    Chops with Balsamic Vinegar, 36
    Chops with Tart Cherries, 37
Turkey Tenderloin, 38-44
    with Anchovy Pesto, 38
    with Cloves and Orange Sauce, 40
    with Fresh Figs and Port Wine Sauce, 41
    with Ginger and Honey Sauce, 42
    with Lemon and Crisp Sage, 43
    Rolls with Blueberries, 39
    with Sweet and Sour Quince, 44

Turnips and Carrots with Parsley and
    Orange, 116
Two-Colored Rice, 107

Vegetable(s), 112–130. *See also* Name of
    Vegetable
    about, 111
    Bulgur Pilaf, 89
    Cabbage Rolls with, 115
    and Champagne Sauce, Chicken Breasts with,
      18
    Chowder en Croûte, 60
    Fragrant, Chicken Thighs with, 21
    Polenta, 108
    Ragout, 128
    -Salmon Terrine with Tomato Dill Sauce, 79
    Stock, 164
    Three, Saffron Risotto with, 102
Vidalia Onions Stuffed with Zucchini, 129

Yellow Tomato Soup with Anchovy Toast, 61

Zucchini
    with Black Quinoa Filling, 130
    and Red Peppers, Hearts of Palm with, 123
    Vidalia Onions Stuffed with, 129